SPIRITISM
IN·THE·ARTS

SPIRITISM IN·THE·ARTS

© Copyright 2018 by the United States Spiritist Council

ISBN 978-1-948109-04-8
LCCN 2018930307
Proofreading: Jussara Korngold
Book design: Helton Mattar Monteiro
Cover design: Mauro de Souza Rodrigues

International data for cataloging in publication (CIP)

D395s   Denis, Léon, 1846-1927
Spiritism in the arts / Léon Denis.
Translator: Helton Mattar Monteiro. – New York: United States Spiritist Council, 2018.
148 pp.; 21.59 cm.

Original title: Le Spiritisme dans l'Art (La Revue Spirite, vol. 65, 1922).

ISBN: 978-1-948109-04-8

Includes appendix.

1. Arts. 2. Music. 3. Spiritism. 4. Massenet, Jules I. Title.

LCCN: 2018930307   DDC 133.93   UDC 133.7

1st edition, 1st print – February 2018

All rights reserved to
United States Spiritist Council
http://www.spiritist.us – info@spiritist.us

Manufactured in the United States of America

No part of this book may be reproduced or transmitted in any form or by any means, electronic or mechanical, including photocopying, recording, or by any information storage and retrieval system, without the prior permission in writing from the copyright holder.

The name "United States Spiritist Federation" is a trade mark registered of the United States Spiritist Council.

Léon Denis

SPIRITISM IN·THE·ARTS

Translated by H. M. Monteiro

UNITED STATES
SPIRITIST FEDERATION
New York
2018

Contents

Foreword VII

1. Architecture and Painting 1
   Lessons of the Esthete 11
   I 11
   II 14

2. Genius and Inspiration 19
   Lessons of the Esthete 27
   III 27
   IV 31

3. The Artistic Sense 37
   Lessons of the Esthete 42
   V 42
   VI 44

4. Literature and Eloquence 47
   Lessons of the Esthete 58
   VII 58
   VIII 63

5. Theater and Music 67
   Lessons of the Esthete 76
   IX 76
   X 80

6. Earthly versus Spiritual Music 85

7. Spiritual Music – five lessons 105

First lesson of Massenet's spirit 106
Lesson Comments 108
Second lesson of Massenet's spirit ..109
Third lesson of Massenet's spirit 112
2nd & 3rd Lesson Comments 114
Fourth lesson of Massenet's spirit ..116
Lesson Comments 120
Fifth lesson of Massenet's spirit 122
Final Comments 125

Appendix – biographies 127
Léon Denis 129
Jules Massenet 135

FOREWORD

In 1922, at the height of his powers and maturity as a thinker, Léon Denis produced an enterprising series of essays called *Spiritism in the Arts*. With chapters titled consistent with their main subjects and footnotes added whenever needed, these were now carefully translated and compiled in book form by the United States Spiritist Federation.

Far from being just a personal inquiry into the artistic scene of the time, this study turned out to be a fully-fledged mediumistic experiment, with Léon Denis consulting a couple of spirits during monthly seances. On the author's own initiative, they offered invaluable information on the subject, which is sometimes quite revelatory in itself.

What makes this book uniquely interesting is its reliance on expert opinion and vivid testimonials by spirit artists now living on the other side.

This not only makes for exciting and enlightening reading but, hopefully, should also provide a superb sample of the author's inspired writing at its best, for he valued art, above all music, very highly.

The importance and relevance of Denis's thought and texts remain unchallenged in the 21st Century. They offer a refreshing respite for the almost uniform pessimism and negativity which seem to have become today's zeitgeist.

USSF

Architecture and Painting

Beauty is one of the divine attributes. God has put in all beings and things this mysterious charm which attracts us, seduces us, captivates us and fills our souls with admiration, sometimes with enthusiasm.

Art is the search, the study, the manifestation of that eternal beauty of which we perceive only a reflection here below. To see it in all its splendor, in all its power, one needs to gradually go up toward its emanating source, which is a difficult task for most of us. At least we can know it through the spectacle offered by the universe to the senses, or through the works it inspires in people of genius.

Spiritism has opened to art new perspectives, limitless horizons. The communication which it has established between the seen and the unseen worlds, the indications given about life conditions in the Hereafter, the revelation it has brought to us concerning higher laws of harmony and beauty which govern the universe, present thinkers and artists with inexhaustible subjects of inspiration.

The observation of phenomena of apparitions gives our painters images of the fluidic life of which the French artist James Tissot had already availed himself in the illustrations of his book *The Life of Our Lord Jesus Christ*.[1] Speakers, writers, poets will find in it a fertile source of ideas and feelings. The knowledge of the successive lives of the soul, with its painful ascent through the centuries, and the teaching of the spirits on this magnificent subject of destiny, will shed an unexpected light over all history, and will also give novelists and poets new themes and lofty inspirations for their works, along with a whole set of intellectual resources that will surpass in wealth all that human thought has known so far.

When one thinks of everything that Spiritism has brought to humanity, and considers the treasures of consolation and hope, the inexhaustible mine of art and beauty that has consistently been offered by it, one cannot feel but pity for those ignorant or treacherous individuals, whose malevolent criticism has no other purpose than to discredit, ridicule and even try to stifle this nascent idea, whose benefits are already so evident. Obviously, this idea, in its application, should require due examination and rigorous control, but the beauty that emerges from it will seem striking to any impartial seeker, any attentive observer.

Materialism, under its withering breath, had sterilized art. It crawled in the basements of realism

---

1 [Trans. note] J. J. Tissot, *The Life of Our Lord Jesus Christ* (Toronto: G. N. Morang, 1899).

without being able to rise to the peaks of ideal beauty. Spiritism gives the latter a new impetus, a more lively impulsion towards the heights, where it can find the fruitful source of inspirations and the sublimity of genius.

The essential purpose of art, as we have said, is the quest for and realization of beauty. It is at the same time the search for God, since God is the first source and the perfect realization of physical and moral beauty.

The more refined, fine tuned, and elevated intelligence becomes, the more it is imbued with the idea of beauty. The essential objective of evolution will therefore be the search for and conquest of beauty in order to realize it in our selves and in its works. Such is the rule of the soul in its infinite ascension.

Already in this we realize the necessity of successive existences as a means of acquiring, through continuous and gradual efforts, an ever more precise sense of good and beauty. Here below, the beginnings are modest, the soul is firstly submitted to humble, obscure, obliterated tasks; then, little by little, as it reaches new stages, the spirit acquires the dignity of an artist. Higher still, it will open up to the vast and deep conceptions which are the privilege of genius, finally becoming able to realize the supreme law of ideal beauty.

On Earth, artists are not all inspired by this higher ideal. Most of them limit themselves to imitating what they call "nature," without realizing that it is only one aspect of the divine work. But on the spiritual plane, art takes on forms that are both more subtle and more magnificent, and that are illuminated with divine reflections.

This is why, in this study, I have been particularly interested in consulting our Spirit Guides, in order to collect and summarize their teachings. On the plane where they live, the sources of inspiration are more abundant, with an ampler field of action; for there the thought, the will and the supreme power assert themselves and radiate more intensely.

Our invisible protectors first sent us the spirit of Massenet[2] who came to teach us five lessons on celestial music, proceeding as he used to do on Earth, in his classes at the Paris Conservatoire. But that could not suffice us; we needed more general data, an overview of how art is understood and practiced in the Hereafter.

In works inspired by spirits, especially in Anglo-Saxon books, one often notices the description of sites, monuments, and dwellings created by means of fluids, through the will of the inhabitants of the spiritual plane. We need clarification on this controversial subject about which precise indications have so far been lacking.[3]

---

[2] [Trans. note] Composer Jules Massenet (1842-1912).

[3] [Trans. note] L. DENIS was writing in 1922, some two decades before many books dictated by Spirit ANDRÉ

After our repeated requests, and in order to keep us informed, our guides announced an entity which presented itself under the name of *l'Esthète* [*the Esthete*], whose true identity would only be revealed to us at the end of this study. We immediately felt to be in the presence of a highly evolved spirit.

This phenomenon occurs in the form of "incorporations."[4] As soon as the entity takes possession of the entranced medium, the features of the latter, who is a blind young man, take on an expression of calm, almost angelic serenity, which greatly contrasts with the manner of being of other spirits. The speech is soft, penetrating and when the session is over, the assistants find themselves under an impression of serene peace and deep tranquility. After waking, the medium completely ignores what has been said through his mouth during trance, and says he has been immersed in a "bath of radiation." He feels an inexpressible sensation of well-being.

The *Esthete* took architecture as the subject of its first two psychographed lessons, which will be reproduced later on in this chapter. He chose the cathedral[5] as a model because it can be used as a setting for all the other arts. Later on, that spirit

---

LUIZ through the mediumship of FRANCISCO C. XAVIER revealed in copious detail the existence of entire cities built in the spiritual world.

[4] [Trans. note] In today's Spiritism, *incorporations* are preferably called *psychophonies* (i.e., *speaking mediumship*), considering that no actual embodiment takes place.

[5] [Translator note:] Gothic cathedrals, as referred here, were masterpieces built all over Europe in the Middle Ages.

talked about sculpture, painting and eloquence. Finally, a study about music and lessons given by Massenet conclude the current presentation.

Let us recall here that every spirit, once emanated from God, is not only in possession of a spark of divine intelligence. They also share a fragment of creative power, a power which they are called to manifest increasingly more during their evolution, both in their planetary incarnations and in their life on the spiritual plane.

On Earth, while veiled by flesh, that intelligence and this power are lessened; and yet is it not marvelous to see to what extent the genius of humans has been able to subjugate the brutal forces of matter, to overcome their resistance, their hostility, to enslave them to their needs and even to their fancies! Human beings forge the iron, melt the bronze and the glass, carve the stone, raise statues, build palaces and temples; we humans drill through mountains and gather the seas together.

But on the spiritual plane this creative power asserts itself with all the more power, since the fluidic matter is much more subtle and, by now, the spirit has learned to better combine the ethereal elements which are the very substance of the universe. There, all the difficulties of earthly work disappear; it suffices to keep a sustained mental action to impart to fluids the forms that the spirit wishes to achieve and render durable.

Even from this life, we can see in hypnotic sleep the will of the operator imparting temporary properties to objects and substances, which exert incontestable influences on the subjects.

To a higher degree, for example in the materializations of spirits, the force of the will of the latter is able to create forms, faces, clothes, attributes similar to those that they possessed on Earth, making it possible to recognize them, to identify them. In these cases, the thought aided by memory recreates objects that were particular to them, such as clothing and weapons. The will provides them with the consistency necessary to strike the senses of observers. There is no point in seeking elsewhere an explanation for these phenomena, which are known to all experienced spiritualists. Our spirit guides assure us that on the spiritual plane the strangest and most varied architectures can be found, or they surpass in size and beauty any creations of our dreams. On this point we have most precise testimonies: the deceased son of Sir Oliver Lodge, Raymond, has reportedly built himself a cottage according to his earthly tastes. The spirits of Mozart, Victorien Sardou and others have built veritable palaces adorned with plants and flowers. We are told that ancient earthly architects, are building shrines where the rites of this or that cult are celebrated. Spirits like to reconstitute environments resembling those they frequented on Earth, yet superior in beauty; and this they do with all the more ease as they can dispose of much more flexible and malleable materials.

These are astonishing stories and descriptions, which have generated many comments However, if we see what happens in experimental seances, with phenomena such as apportation,[6] levitation, penetration of matter by matter, disintegration and reconstitution of objects through walls, all these demonstrate the power of spirits over fluids and should facilitate our understanding. Some psychists admit that they know nothing about it, thus showing their lack of practice in Spiritism, while mere sympathizers are perfectly aware of these facts.

Now let us return to architecture, which the *Esthete* took as the subject of its first lessons. Already, down here on Earth, it is the sublime art to which all the other arts are attached, and which often serves them as a shelter.

As on Earth, music represents the living art, mobile and vibrant harmony, whereas architecture represents immobile and passive art in its imposing and rigid forms. But while within the spaces the spirit models the fluidic material at will, gives it the appearances, hues, outlines as it wishes, on our planet matter opposes more resistance to the human

---
[6] [Trans. note] *Apportation* or *apports* are the same as "teleportation" of objects in modern parlance.

will. The stone block resists the sculptor's chisel and the mason's tool. Sometimes it takes long and patient efforts, and persistent toil, for the expression of beauty in marble and granite.

The Esthete's lessons highlight the difference between the processes used on Earth and those in the spiritual world, when it comes to achieve artistic creations. While on Earth, the cathedral, taken as an architectural type, is the result of patient and lasting work by a working collectivity, from the humble stonemason to the great artist who drew the overall plan. Conversely, on the spiritual plane, it is the particular work of a master that, instantly and at will, can build or destroy it, assisted only by a group of students who seek to assimilate and imitate their master's creative thinking. Here below the monument is the work of a human crowd, the labor of centuries. For generations, artists and workmen have worked together to raise these columns, spires and towers, melting and molding these windows, painting these images, and carving these statues. Thus the pyramids, the palaces and the cathedrals were slowly gaining form. That is why in their majestic unity they symbolize the spirit of a people, the genius of a race, the soul of a religion.

It is faith, enthusiasm and an ardent spirituality that have raised these veritable Bibles of stone to heaven. And in these colossal works, the unseen have their role; they think with the architect, meditate with the artist, act with and through the craftsman. In all they inspire the thought of God and the

Hereafter, to the extent that they can understand and interpret it.

Thus were built these imposing "books," these cathedrals which, for centuries, have sufficed to guide, instruct, and comfort the human spirit. The earthly cathedral serves as a framework for all the arts. Music makes its vast naves vibrate, paintings decorate its walls, sculpture adorn it with statues. Yet, as a whole, it still keeps the cold immobility and opacity of granite.

The essential role of art is to express life in all its power, through grace and beauty. Yet life is movement. And it is precisely in this that lies the main difficulty of human art, which can reproduce movement only through music. The other arts can only give the illusion. The sculptor, by the attitude he imparts to his statue, renders the movement that his thought conceives, and creates motion in immobility. A painting may give the same impression by means of a gesture fixed on the canvas, and through the harmony of colors, the play of perspectives, the simulation of depths and distant horizons. There is more force in statues and more artifice in paintings; yet both can express the ideal beauty in the form of masterpieces known to us. However, in spite of the brilliant intention that has presided over their execution, they never give us anything but sensations of beauty.

This is not what happens to the works of art built on the spiritual plane: everything is life, movement, color, and light. The fluidic cathedral will be animated and alive. Its columns will have the suppleness and the elasticity of the most subtle matter, its walls will be translucent as crystal, and a thousand hues unknown on Earth will play in shifting networks of shadow and light. All harmonies are combined in waves of inexpressible sweetness; and everything vibrates with the thrill of intense and deep life.

Artists of the Earth ought to take inspiration from these superhuman models that Spiritist teachings will make familiar to them. Human aesthetic education will entail higher and higher conceptions so that the sense of beauty penetrates and grows in all souls. Already an evolution has been occurring in this respect, it will be accentuated under the influence of the Hereafter. The artists of the future will strive to give more fluidity to colors, more life to marble, more spirituality to all their works. The complementary arts will be idealized while leaving to architecture the majesty of rigid forms and the illusion of immutability in stillness.

Art enhances itself and progresses at every single step of life's ladder, accomplishing ever more noble and perfect forms as it approaches the divine source of eternal beauty.

LESSONS OF THE ESTHETE
I

I am glad to talk about an art that was the subject of my constant concern. You are a hundred times right in defending the cause of art and putting it in parallel on Earth and on the spiritual plane. Art is of divine essence, it is a manifestation of the thought of God, a radiation of the brain and the heart of God transmitted in the artistic form.

However, many things of the divine plan cannot be transmitted to humans. Art, in the form of inspiration, is part of that wonderful whole that makes up the universe. It is the lightning, or rather the spark, that establishes the rapport between God and creation.

You may wonder what are the reflexes of art that we keep, after having lived series of existences in different worlds. I will try to tell you.

On Earth, art does not amount to much and you seem satisfied with it. Yet, art exists in all domains: in the domain of thought, of sculpture, of music. It is in the latter that it manifests itself best and becomes accessible to a larger number of brains. First of all, when the human spirit incarnates on Earth bringing with it, either from its life on the spiritual plane, or as a result of previous work during earthly lives, a certain notion of esthetic ideal, as soon as the incarnate reaches maturity in its earthly life, his or her artistic background is exteriorized in the form of inspirations along with a key, central quality that

I will call taste, which for its turn is connected to a sense of beauty. So this is how an artist is born and ready to work on matter.

Upon accomplishing a lifetime of work, the artist returns to the spiritual plane. Once arriving there, a multitude of thoughts emerge from the artist who will then wish to concretize them. In this fluidic environment, the artist will find all the necessary materials to reconstitute what thoughts and ideas imprisoned in flesh could not make real in a single existence.

The mind does not have a visual organ, but thought unites all the senses. First of all, the spirit sees in its memory the most beautiful things that struck its brain in its previous existence. If it has lived in a high-minded environment, thanks to acquired directives, the paintings that will pass through its mind will be truly inspired by the cult of beauty. Therefore, its spiritual being, through its work, will soon be transported into a fluidic environment that is sufficiently pure, free from material particles; and from there it can receive, through memory, the artistic reflection of its previous lives. By a simple wish, everything will be concretized with the help of ambient fluids. Was this spirit a painter? Then its thoughts will reflect the paintings of the masters it has known and loved. Was it a sculptor? Ancient or classical forms, or those of its contemporaneous time will appear on the screen of its thoughts. Then, in the long run, other minds, not attracted by art but eager to rise to a higher plane, will group themselves around beings that, by their work and advancement, hover in purer fluidic regions. These beings, who approach the artist, will more easily receive the thought of the latter; by means of a prolonged work, a fusion will be established between the spirit of the profane and the spirit of the artist. Little by little, the laypersons will receive in their thought the paintings and the artistic scenes of their spiritual master, and will then be able to enjoy very great esthetic joys, and become artists themselves in a future existence, for they will have drawn the first elements of art in contact with a being more advanced than themselves.

Thus, generally speaking, artistic circles are perpetuated from Earth onto the spiritual plane, from the spiritual plane back to Earth and other worlds, because there are many spheres where the means of artistic creation are richer than on your globe.

I must add that spirits, through exchanges of thoughts, can create shapes using the range of colors which is infinite in space: the loftier the plans, the more complex the gamut of colors.

In the Earth's atmosphere, one cannot exteriorize thoughts in a clear and precise way. It is as if you projected your thoughts onto a grayish screen instead of a blank one.

Sometimes spirits meet one another, exchange shapes and forms through their thoughts, and create a variety of pictures and scenes. If there is among them a spirit that has lived in a higher world, it makes its less privileged fellow spirits benefit from the artistic resources it has been able to acquire. The creator of these scenes has the power to destroy immediately what its thought has created. These paintings and scenes are therefore transient and personal to the spirit; but those that have the desire to rise can take advantage of this artistic projection, formed by a combination of fluidic molecules drawn from the ambient environment.

(November 15, 1921)

II

After giving the description of artistic scenes that we record on the spiritual plane, it will be interesting for you to know how we group the elements of these scenes so as to compose works in virtual mode.

I should try to make you understand how we bring together the necessary molecules so that our will can project fluids capable of transforming itself into works that symbolize beauty in all its forms. These works will be felt and perceived by other fluidic beings besides the creators.

Immaterial beings that float in infinitely rich and subtle fluidic regions, have arrived there only after a long and progressive evolution, in which they themselves acquired sufficient knowledge and skills for artistic creation in the worlds where they lived during their human lifetimes.

Let us take an example. A great sculptor, a great painter or a great artist has recently "escaped" from Earth. This artist is still under the impression of the works composed during a previous existence; when its spirit has arrived the spiritual plane, its mind no longer being compressed by matter, it can see the road that it has traveled since the day it received the divine creative essence and **became sure** *that it can, in new existences, develop and complete what you can call its* **genius particle**.

This artist will see unfolding on the spiritual plane all the highlights that have led to the blossoming of its inspiration.

If the spirit was an architect or sculptor, immediately at will, its memory will retrace the monuments or works of art that it created.

I admitted that it hovers in this environment of which I have just spoken. After an appeal to God, the artist's thoughts will find, by their radiations, sufficient fluids to reconstitute all of its works. If these possess a real character of beauty, if the inspiration is pure and the ideal high, the other beings that surround the artist will feel awaken in them a desire for emulation; then little by little, the material veil having been lifted, their personal thought will be fertilized by that of the artist.

Thus a great master sculptor will revive these beautiful monuments in which the Glory of the Most High was sung for centuries. Huge cathedrals are thus rebuilt; but artists do not always limit themselves to the work they have created, their distant vision also recovers the works of their disciples and sometimes their inspiration goes on in the spiritual world to form new works borrowing from various authors the most successful parts of their designs. If you enter the spiritual world, on the high plane of which I speak, you might realize that monuments that are not similar to those erected on your world are reconstructed by the fluidic thinking of beings inspired by God.

The supreme Creator gives each of its children an animating particle that becomes external when the cult of beauty and lofty ideals awaken in them. Our religious monuments become living images there. Are not these bold spires darting to the sky a faithful representation of the thought of humans flying in ultimate prayer to that God which created us? Whether it is a cathedral or a temple of antiquity; whether in Greece, in Rome, in Florence or in your own country, seek and you will always find that a higher thought presides over the hatching of architectural works.

A small comparison, perhaps moving away from my subject: If you consider the history of Architecture in Germany in these modern times, you will find that the elevation to the sky is absent, that massive and square shapes have replaced the dome or the ogive; thought creeps on Earth and no longer flies to the divine.

In painting, study the Florentine school at the time of the Renaissance, and you will find that when the works have a mystical character, the features are divinized and the scenes take on a character of real beauty and true grandeur.

It is the same with all the arts. For example, does not sacred music have a character that touches more closely to the divine, while profane music, when it comes close to materialism, takes a character of low and crude realism?

(*November 22, 1921*)

Genius and Inspiration

As said in the previous chapter, art in its various forms is the expression of eternal beauty, a manifestation of the powerful harmony that governs the universe; it is the ray from above that dissipates the mists, the obscurities of matter, giving us a glimpse of the plans of the higher life. It is itself rich in teachings, revelations, and light. It brings the soul to the regions of spiritual life, which is its true life that it aspires to find one day.

Well-thought-out art is a powerful means of elevation and self-renewal. It is the source of the most pure enjoyments; it beautifies life, sustains and comforts us when going through ordeals, and traces in advance the roads to heaven. When sustained, inspired by sincere faith and noble ideals, art is always a fertile source of instruction, and an incomparable means of civilization and perfection.

Yet all too often nowadays it is degraded, diverted from its purpose, enslaved to petty theories of certain schools of thought, which considers it above all as a means of arriving at fortune, with earthly honors. It is being used to flatter evil passions and excite the senses, thus being turned into an instrument of self-debasement.

Almost all those who received the sacred mission of leading souls to the highest summits have evaded this task. They have been guilty of a crime, by refusing to instruct and enlighten societies, thus perpetuating the moral disorder and all the evils that underlie humanity. This should explain the decadence of art in our days and the absence of imposing works.

The thought of God is source of high and healthy inspirations. If our artists knew how to draw from it, they would find the secret of imperishable works and the higher felicities of art. Through Spiritism they are offered the spiritual resources need by our time in order to regenerate itself. It makes us understand that life, in all its fullness, is nothing other than the conception and the realization of eternal beauty.

To live is to always rise, always grow, and always increase in oneself the feeling and the sense of beauty.

Great works of art can only be elaborated in recollection and silence, at the cost of long meditations and more or less conscious communion with the higher spheres. The din of cities is not suited to the expansion of thought; on the contrary, the calm of nature, the deep peace of the mountains, should facilitate inspiration and encourage the blossoming of genius, once again confirming this old Arabic proverb: "Noise be to humans, silence to God."

Every Spiritist knows of the immense help provided by communion with the Hereafter, with its heavenly spirits, to artists, writers, and poets. Almost all great works have had invisible contributors. This association is strengthened and accentuated by faith and prayer. These allow forces from above to penetrate deeper into us and permeate our whole being. More than any other, Spiritists feel those powerful currents passing through pensive fronts and inspiring ideas, forms, harmonies that are like materials employed by a genius to compose a superb work.

The awareness of such cooperation gives the measure of our weakness; it makes us understand how much is due to the influence of our elder fellow beings, of our spirit guides, of those who, from the spiritual plane, bend over us and assist us in our work. It teaches us to be humble in success. It is human pride that has dried up the source of high inspiration. Vanity, which is a defect of many artists, dries their minds and drives away great souls that otherwise would consent to protect them. Pride creates a barrier between us and the powers of the Hereafter.

Spiritist artists admit their own indigence, but know that above them lies a boundless world, full of riches and incalculable treasures near which all the resources of the Earth are only poverty and misery. Spiritists also know that this unseen world, provided they know how to make themselves worthy of it by purifying their thought and heart, can make more intense the action from the On High, letting them participate in its riches through inspiration and revelation, allowing works to be like a reflection of the higher life and divine glory.

The main purpose of this chapter is to show the considerable role played by inspiration at all times in the evolution of art and thought. All students of the occult know that a flood of ideas, forms, and images is constantly pouring out of the unseen world over humanity. Most writers, artists, poets, inventors, are aware of these powerful currents, which come to fertilize their brains, to widen the circle of their conceptions.

Sometimes, inspiration slips gently into our intellect, mixing intimately with our own thought, in such a way that it becomes impossible to distinguish it. At other times, it is like a sudden irruption, a cerebral invasion, a breath that passes through our foreheads and shakes us with a sort of fever. Other times still, it is like an inner voice, so crisp and clear that it seems to come from without, to speak to us of deep and profound things. A current of forces and thoughts are moving and rolling around us, seeking to penetrate human brains willing to receive, assimilate and translate them into forms and shapes, to the extent of their capacities, their degree of evolution. Some will express them in a more ample manner, others, more restricted according to their aptitudes, and according to the richness or the poverty of expression familiar to them, and the resources of their respective intellects.

The lessons given by the spirit '*the Esthete*,' reproduced later on, will specify the various types of inspiration according to each case.

Many individuals of genius have acknowledged these invisible influences. Several describe a state close to trance, which plunges them into the elaboration of a great work. Others speak of the burning flow that penetrates them, of the fire that runs in their veins and provokes overexcitement that multiply their faculties a hundredfold. In vain do they sometimes seek to resist that power which dominates them, subjugates them, and that would break their envelope if it were continuous. There are those who succumbed to this sovereign action and died prematurely, like Renaissance painter and architect Raphael, then at the prime of his life.

Lamartine depicted this state in famous verses:[7]
Yet to the rise of thought, in vain
The instincts of the senses oppose.
Under this god my soul thus burdened
Springs up, takes over, and beats on my breast.
The lightning now circulates in my veins.
Astonished by the fire that burns me,
I fight it out, consequently enraging it;
Then the lava of my genius,
Overflowing in torrents of harmony,
Consumes me, as it escapes through.

---
[7] Alphonse de LAMARTINE (Méditation XI, "l'Enthousiasme").

The biographer Romain Rolland describes in the following terms the special case of Michelangelo (*Revue de Paris*, 1906, and *Cahiers de la Quinzaine*):

"The strength of genius from the hidden God is more clearly manifested in a man without will, such as Michelangelo. Never was man such a prey for it. This genius did not seem similar to him; it was a conqueror that had rushed into him and kept him enslaved. His own will availed him nothing and we could almost say, neither did his spirit or his heart. It was a frenzied exaltation, a great life in a body and soul too weak to contain it."

We find in Goethe (*Goethe's Correspondence with a Child*) the following details about Beethoven:

"Beethoven, speaking of the source whence came the conception of his masterpieces, once said to Bettina: 'I feel myself compelled to let the melody stream forth on all sides – I follow it – passionately overtake it again – I see it escape me, vanish amidst the crowd of varied excitements – soon I seize upon it again with renewed passion; I cannot part from it, – with quick rapture I multiply it in every form of modulation – and at the last moment I triumph over the first musical thought ...'"

"I have to live alone with myself; but I know well that God is closer to me in my art than to all others, and I advance with him without fear, having recognized and understood him every time. Nor do I feel anxious about my music which could have no adverse destiny: he who freely opens his mind and his feelings shall be forever exempt from all the misery in which the others drag along."

Mozart, for his part, in one of his letters to a close friend, introduces us to the mysteries of musical inspiration. The following letter was first published by Edward Holmes, in his *Life of Mozart, including his Correspondence* (London, 1845).

"You say you should like to know my way of composing, and what method I follow in writing works of some extent. I can really say no more on this subject than the following, for I myself know no more about it, and cannot account for it."

"When I am, as it were, completely myself, entirely alone, and of good cheer ... it is on such occasions that my ideas flow best and most abundantly. *Whence* and *how* they come, I know not, nor can I force them."

Schiller declared that his finest thoughts were not of his own creation; they came to him so quickly and with such force that he had difficulty grasping them quickly enough to transcribe them.

Michelet, at certain hours, also seemed to have been under the control of some unknown power. Speaking of his book *History of the Revolution*, he said:

"Never since my Maid of Orleans [Joan of Arc] had I had such a ray from above, such a luminous escape from heaven ..."

"Unforgettable days; who am I to have narrated them? I do not know yet, I will never know how I could reproduce them. The incredible happiness of recovering them so palpitating with life, so burning, after sixty years, had enlarged my heart with heroic joy."

The power of inspiration is translated by Henri Heine in an even more tangible way. This is what he said in the preface to his tragedy, *W. Ratcliff*:

"I wrote *William Ratcliff* in Berlin during the last days of 1821, under the lime trees of the Lidernallee, while the sun was shining with its rather dull rays over the roofs covered with snow, and the trees were stripped of their leaves. I wrote without interruption and without deletions. As I wrote, it seemed to me that I could hear something like a rustle of wings above my head."

Quotations of the same kind could be multiplied, showing that inspiration varies according to the artist's nature. In some, the brain acts like a mirror, reflecting hidden things and sending back radiation to humanity. Under a thousand forms, it penetrates sensitives and imposes itself.

Next, the two lessons (III and IV) of the *Esthete* that we are about to read are based on this subject, considering its cause and general effects, both on Earth and the spiritual world.

In our seances, these lessons continue regularly each week, but we still do not know the real name and personality of this entity. However, we notice that the familiar spirits of our group make way respectfully and remain silent before this spirit alone. The medium's spirit guide comes after the departure of the *Esthete*, to utter some words of friendship and encouragement, while confessing to be "embarrassed by the superiority and the radiance of this great spirit."

Whatever the value of the writing form itself, we wanted to faithfully reproduce the author's thought, carefully avoiding anything that could have altered its meaning, even to the detriment of style.

Lessons of the Esthete

III

I would like to talk to you about inspiration. It is a process of transmission of the divine spark occurring in various forms, since art, with its multiple sectors, approaches at various different degrees this divine plane of which I speak to you. When from the spiritual plane, the spirit of an artist decides to reincarnate, it takes with itself the friendships of loved ones that, for various reasons, must remain on the spiritual plane. However, through intuition, these friends will send to this being now imprisoned in the flesh, fluids coming from their environment and ideas that will give a new impetus to the latter's genius particle that is in it and that could be too willing to sleep under the flesh. Inspiration has two forms: one personal, the other broader, transmitted by higher order spirits, who draw art from the purest sources and communicate its effects to a being who is capable to implement them by his or her own natural means.

Personal inspiration is the most frequent. You are aware that a being who is capable of experiencing this phenomenon has already evolved; its evolution will have occurred gradually. In each of this being's lifetimes, there will have been a period which was more marked than the others, the one where the work has been more obstinate and, consequently, more productive; this will result in acquisitions that will accumulate in its perispirit. In the next life, these acquisitions will reappear, in the form of a native gift. This gift, for the uninitiated, will be named as inspiration. But this inspiration has only a human character, it is generally cold, not being animated by divine sparks.

To make this inspiration more beautiful, loftier, it must be impregnated with ideals and fluids emanating from the divine source. Thus we come to the second form of inspiration. You are aware that invisible friends watch over sentient beings that they feel are worthy of protection and encouragement. From the spiritual plane, higher order spirits can sense the small flame engendered by personal inspiration. To make it brighter, by prayer, if God allows it, these guides will draw on spheres where wonderful radiations reign, elements of creative life, which will feed this little flame and make the sparks of genius burst forth.

It may happen that the human body is a little troubled by these forces. Whenever the physical atoms cannot withstand this influx, there is some disorder in the body. This explains why men of genius sometimes lack balance.

Here is the material explanation of the phenomenon. What will the being feel under the breath of an inspiration? If the being is sensitive enough, when an idea, a thought that it could not foresee, strikes its brain, it will assimilate it like a telephone receiver that receives electric waves and vibrates as they pass through. Is this being a painter? Suddenly, on its palette, it will find the secret of the mixture of powders, which will produce a new color, adapting admirably to the play of physiognomy or the highlight to be imparted to a painting in progress. Is it a thinker, a writer, a poet? From this same brain will spring the idea, the image, the expression that must enhance and illustrate the work, which needs to take on a higher and more colorful form. Is it a musician? At the moment when the being least expects it, a chord, a harmonic series, a melody will come to lend, by their mellowness, purity and richness, to the musician's composition an emphasis that it could otherwise not have acquired. If, from birth, the human being is in love with high ideals, you can imagine the new treasures that will be attached to it. Ideal art is one of the forms of prayer, its thought will attract very highly evolved invisible friends; and it will be much easier for them to enhance the brilliancy of the flame which was lit up early on; and from the artist's soul will spring up works inspired by what is divine and beautiful.

In general, an artist must remain in a healthy environment, because the creative flame that animates him or her can be extinguished under the influence of a fluidic atmosphere charged with material molecules. True art does not seek the enjoyments of the table, of the flesh, or pleasures in which the spirit and the higher brain have no part.

In your country, France, you have had wonderful artists, who have created admirable works in every field. Those of the Italian Renaissance were, I must tell you, a pleiad inspired by no less great artists from the spiritual plane. These artists of the Renaissance had found their creative source in Greek and Latin antiquity. After living in Greece, Egypt and Rome, they returned to the spiritual world. There, their knowledge was enlarged, they acquired a polish, a totally particular style and, when they reincarnated, they left the paganism to celebrate, in all its aspects, the glory of God, of which they had impregnated themselves at the end of their last stay in the celestial spheres. Their previous lives on Earth had been devoted to basic work, that is to say, the preparation of this little flame that was to become like an attracting pole of the divine essence. That is why the work of the painters, sculptors and musicians of this period has this tinge of piety, sweetness and tranquility that you do not find in the current time.

In my next talk I will try to tell you something about inspiration in this day and age. It is also beautiful in some cases, but its characteristics are not the same. Current inspiration, in which new points of view are mingled, should help a general transformation of humanity through an evolution of thought, by drawing nearer to and communicating with the unseen world, the intermediate of the divine plane.

(November 29, 1921)

IV

I would like to talk about inspiration in modern times. You should understand that there are three great stages: initiation, work, and progression. The blossoming, while partial on the worlds, is complete in the spiritual world. We have seen our artists make their initiation in antiquity, either in Greece, Egypt or Rome. Back in the spiritual world, these beings have matured and put to good use the qualities acquired in a material environment; once returned to Earth in another incarnation, they brought their ideal to the time of the Renaissance, then this ideal flourished a century later in the literature, the arts, and the architecture. I would to like to talk about the century of Louis XIV. After these spirits returned to the spiritual world for a long time, inspiration in general was but mediocre in the 18th century and latent in the 19th.

What specifically is inspiration nowadays?

Spirits, imbued with the beautiful works gleaned on Earth and in the spiritual world, being currently discarnate, will return at a time when divinized art and spirit will have blossomed again in a more intense way. At the same time, other spirits, that have worked on material evolution in previous lives, have currently imbued themselves with positivism and, here below, their inspiration, which can be classified as a form of personal inspiration, is moving toward scientific goals. Yet the group of idealist artists who remain on the spiritual plane, seeks to illuminate with a divine light those beings who have good qualities, from the point of view of work, and who must bring forth the spark of science.

This is why, at this moment, you notice a struggle between pure science and the search for human destinies, their formation and that of the Cosmos.

You may ask: How art is conceived on the spiritual plane? Art springs from inspiration, so it was necessary to show you how art develops and grows into a constant evolution, so that you can realize the ascending march of spirituality. Only when you understand how the artistic spark, the divine spark, emerges from the mind, you will also be able to understand and idealize the paintings that take place on the spiritual plane, more magnificent, and more accomplished than those that you see on Earth, which are only their pale reflection.

Positivist spirits on Earth, bearers of a creative spark, seek to unveil the mystery of life and the universe, through the scientific inspiration that is characteristic of them, plus the one they receive from discarnate beings.

All forces intertwine, from the visible world to the invisible world. The idealistic spirits, from above, seek to animate with a flame that will spiritualize them, the beings that have worked in different epochs, and that have thus acquired a personal inspiration, albeit cold and rigid.

Scientific spirits of your time did not live at the same period as the idealists who designed such beautiful works; and that is why, from the spiritual plane, they seek to ignite scientists. Their personal inspiration is confined to a field that touches matter. Their creative spark reaches only the brain, not the soul. It was therefore necessary that great initiating spirits came from the spiritual plane in order to breathe on your contemporaries the great inspiration that very slowly leads them, through material examples, to the revelation of unknown forces.

Hertzian waves[8] are one of the concrete forms of fluidic currents, created by God and transmitted by spirits. The first human, who, in the form of an inspiration, ascertained their existence, arrived at this conclusion little by little with the help of the invisible, that wished to reveal to the inhabitants of the Earth the power of currents unknown to them. But from scientific inspiration to idealistic inspiration there is a gap. Difficulties crop up because of different means of action, yet, in future centuries, all beings should vibrate in unison, and currently, the fulcrum of scientific researchers needs to feel an inspiration, where science and the spiritualized form of divine work mingle in all their grandeur and beauty. Since the waves of living beings that dwell

---

[8] [Transl. note] Former term for *radio waves*.

on Earth have not all reached the same degree of evolution, the inspiration that animates each wave cannot be of the same nature. In order to prepare the progressive task of generations, there is in scientific inspiration a mixture of the unknown, the surprise which sometimes engenders a skepticism which will not last for long.

Inevitably, there will be a time in the cycle which is being prepared, when your scientists will have to accept and teach to your humanity the new forces which spring continually from the ether. The day in which your scientists will have discovered, through intuition and inspiration, the source of the currents that animate the universe, the divine ideal will be ready to blossom again on Earth; and we can affirm, with you, that Earth's evolution will have taken a big step. Scientific evolution continues in all fields, from precious material discoveries to the application of positivist and new principles to the arts. Currently your arts, excepting literature, proceed in a somewhat impulsive manner of impression and inspiration. If, during the Renaissance, the compositions sometimes seemed a little naive, in your day, the color, the form, the power of inspiration are not lacking, but it will be necessary to acquire in future centuries the notion of the ideal that will serve as a link to all works of thought. Through it, God gives you the real and profound meaning of his universal work.

In this study, we have seen the brain of the artist organized in all areas. Inspiration, whether it comes *from the personality or from the divine ideal, is the form that concretizes art. Incarnate beings acquire it on Earth, their spirits complete it in the spiritual world.*

Later on, I will review the beautiful conceptions that can reflect from an ardent soul at work with full admiration for the Creator.

(December 5, 1921)

The Artistic Sense

What is the artistic sense, after all? An attentive study of the soul shows us that everything in nature – sounds, scents, rays, colors – find in us their correspondences, their analogies, and that their radiations blend and harmonize with the depths of one's own self, depending on the extent of one's evolution. This is what constitutes the so-called artistic sense, the understanding of beauty in all its forms.

The evolution of this inner sense and the faculty of expressing it will develop from lifetime to lifetime, until the soul ends up producing talent, genius. In the high aspects of art, the artist finds a higher conception of eternal beauty; the artist understands that its only source comes from God. This source pours itself into the infinite expanse for infinity, onto all beings, penetrating them according to their degree of receptivity.

Rays and colors, sounds and scents, are all connected in sequence, a kind of range in which each note represents a particular sum of vibrations, and which constitute as a whole one perfect unity.

If we add forms and lines to it, this unity becomes the general law of beauty; and art, in its multiple manifestations, will have for object to replicate them.

The study of art and its achievements gradually permeate the splendors of the universe. At first deaf and unconscious in primitive humans, this work becomes conscious, accentuates, reveals itself in soaring forms, until it becomes as a reflection of the supreme beauty.

Yet, on Earth, art is stammering. On the other worlds, and especially on the spiritual plane – so say our spirit guides – it gives birth to wonders near which the most beautiful human works would appear very poor and almost childish by comparison. Once arriving at such heights, art becomes the most sublime form of worship rendered to divinity.

So far the artist has been inspired by the things of the visible or tangible world; artists have listened to voices, to harmonies; have studied forms, colors, and have managed to impregnate their works with them. Artists have thus created, between humans and nature, closer and deeper communion. Thanks to artists, the obscure and mute things gained a soul, and their vague aspirations, their complaints, their pains, found expressions which, by making them more alive, brought them closer to us, at the same time as the human soul became more sensitive to the contact with external life.

In this way, art has restored to life in the world the deep meaning it lacked. Through it, the blind powers of nature have penetrated into us and acquired something like a reflection of our consciousness and our feelings. The human soul has gone up to things, and its influence has lent them a more intense mode of life and sensations. Through this communion the soul of the earth has risen to the knowledge of itself, of its role, and of its great destiny. Now, as we can see by the lessons of the *Esthete*, it is quite another world that opens up to ourselves, it is a whole unknown life that arises, richer, more abundant, more varied than all that we had known until now; and art will find in this unknown environment inexhaustible sources of inspiration and poetry, unsuspected forms of thought and life.

Already, the domain of subtle matter and fluids have opened up, revealing itself in its prestigious aspects, offering humankind the means of study and observation which extend to infinity the field of its researches and scientific knowledge. The apparitions of spirits have familiarized us with all these forms of extraterrestrial existence on Earth, from the most dense and coarse spirit materializations to manifestations of the most ideal and radiant life.

Through our regular dialogues with our Spirit Guides, we can obtain indications about life on the spiritual plane, about its magnificent shapes and colors, about its sweet and powerful harmonies, which open to the musician, the colorist, the sculptor, multiple possibilities still unexplored.

Those who enjoy mediumistic faculties will be able to perceive them directly, thus enriching all the resources of art. The vast world of the spirits will become increasingly accessible to our senses, by the spectacles and teachings that it reserved for us. The intellectual powers of humankind will be augmented a hundredfold, and its artistic genius will bring forth works that will surpass all that were achieved in centuries past.

In short, the eternal law of the universe, the sublime purpose of creation, is the fusion of good and beauty. These two principles are inseparable, they inspire all the divine work and constitute the essential basis of the harmonies of the Cosmos.

Thought, since the divine intention is good, manifests itself in beauty. Every being, in its ascent, will have to pervade itself more and more with this sovereign thought, with this will, and endeavor to realize it inside and outside itself, in ever more perfect forms. Happiness should consist in assimilating this law and accomplishing it. The deep inner joys that will result from this are an obvious demonstration of the universe's goal; joys, say the spirits, that human speech is powerless to define. These laws, this essential goal, Spiritism, not only teaches us, but also indicates to us the means of attaining and practicing them. From this standpoint, their role is considerable and their intervention, at the current time in history, providential.

For one century we have witnessed a colossal development in industry and its inventions, with the discovery and application of the physical resources of the globe. Hence, in the realm of ideas, a powerful materialistic current, which gave a new impulse to our appetites, has brought about a pressing desire for well-being and enjoyment. The need is felt, more and more, to oppose a Spiritualist counter-influence to this situation.

Material evolution requires a parallel evolution, both philosophical and religious, without which the intellectual powers would increasingly turn toward evil, and the world would collapse in a cataclysm whose last war[9] would be only the prelude to further destruction.

Above our current lifetime, which is only transitory, it is necessary, in all things, to bear in mind the other life, which is its goal and its sanction. It is only through an ultimate agreement among sciences, philosophies and the more advanced religions that thought will be able to reach the highest peaks, and humanity will regain confidence and peace, with the knowledge of essential truths under their various guises.

---

[9] [Trans. note] At this point the author is prophetically referencing World War II (1939–1945), which had not yet begun.

Lessons of the Esthete

V

In previous lessons I spoke of different degrees of inspiration capable of exteriorizing themselves and of forming scenes, spiritual images made concrete to the beings who inhabit your world and various points of the ether.

After having shown in preliminary lessons how this cerebral gymnastics is accomplished whether unconsciously or consciously in each organized being, I shall now review the phenomenon which, upon a soul's return to the spiritual world, makes these same fluidic beams move reflexively, stored as they were in the form of knowledge in your fleshly envelopes.

For instance, a sculptor has returned to life on the spiritual plane. He or she sees all their past existences, in general the latter had as their center of work (center in the absolute sense of the word), places where nature itself incites beauty. On the spiritual plane, this being cannot turn aways its mind from the thoughts, the visions of the works created by its fellow beings or by itself. Instinctively, its spirit will still soar around monuments and statues that it loved to contemplate during its material life. If its existence took place in such and such country, it will come back to it; if a previous existence occurred in another, the spirit will be instinctively drawn to it by its recollections. At rest, on the spiritual plane, it will enjoy real bliss, and it will project in rays of all colors, scenes and sculptural forms of the most marvelous effect. It can combine Greek, Roman, Latin and Gallic arts, and thus relive unforgettable hours. All the periods of its art will be represented, according to the duration and the types of developments achieved.

One day, in the astral environment where it is, which is composed of special molecules, this spirit will want to make less advanced fellow spirits profit from its most beautiful projections. With the help of a few friends, its thought will beseech God to attract profane spirits who have the desire to rise up, but whose artistic knowledge is still mediocre. In your Earthly terms, it will attempt to "popularize" its art and call to itself an audience of distinguished beings that are undoubtedly distinguished, albeit very little erudite. The inventive spirit of our artists will form porticoes and vaults, combining Greek art with Roman art, and Roman art with ogival art and whatever may form graceful monuments. These fluidically built monuments, borrowing from relatively solid molecules – not that anyone can collide with them – these molecules, for spirits passing by, produce in them an impression close to ecstasy.

The fluidic beings can thus be in presence of architectures that your geometry, still very limited, cannot help me explain.

These works of art may remain fixed on the spiritual plane, lasting for as long as the artist's will wishes; however it feels that its pride has limits: at a given moment, its will instinctively project another picture and the previous monument will disappear, restoring to the azure its former limpidity, until a new work is produced and erected as a replacement.

The molecules that compose these architectural works are in themselves malleable, since they are borrowed from the astral matter; but the thought of the artist, like, incidentally, all the other feelings, makes them iridescent with such colors that all the beings that contemplate these works experience sensations all the more vivid as their elevation is more accentuated.

Models are borrowed either from memories of Earth or other more or less advanced worlds. I will talk about such worlds at the end of these lessons.

If sculpture is interesting, so is painting . There is a gradation among sculpture, painting, music and the art of speech, or written or spoken philosophy.
(January 10, 1922)

VI

After having spoken in our last conversation of architecture on the spiritual plane, today I will focus on painting. There is a marked difference between written and spoken thought, and architecture and painting. Architecture strikes the senses, painting strikes the mind even more than the senses.

In ordinary life, painting is the exact reproduction, as far as possible, of the scenes and settings that God willed to put under our eyes, on the worlds that it has created. Architecture is as much part of inspiration as it is of genius, as well as of the work of human beings. Painting proceeds differently, it tends to fix on any surface the impressions transmitted to the brain by means of receptivity of images.

In your world, paintings will also be inspired by previous visions collected by the artist, either on the spiritual plane or in the worlds the artist has inhabited or visited. Any being that has worked especially in this art, will possess all the necessary materials to reconstitute, in a suitable fluidic environment, the paintings evoked by its thought. Your earth colors form a very incomplete palette, since apart from those represented by nature, you are obliged to create artificial ones using your chemistry.

In the Hereafter, thought is concretized in light beams, taking on the most varied hues. Each thought is therefore reflected in a brilliant trail, more or less colored, in keeping with its orientation.

You understand that it is very easy for a being that already possess, through its evolution, an artistic past, to reproduce in the fluidic environment, not only architectural arcades, but also panels on which it will come to imprint scenes restoring what I may call **the dream in colors.**

In the very spirit of one's being, the colors exist in a latent state, since they themselves are formed of variously colored molecules. These molecules are comparable to small particles of different colored glass. Thinking through these molecules will create a projection reproducing the subjects that haunt it.

Color photography can be used as a comparison, since in a very limited way, it can give a pale idea of fluidic coloring of space.

From thence you can see the diversity of scenes that can be projected by specially organized beings. Naturally it is those who have worked in painting who are able to project the most beautiful paintings, for they possess the harmony of line and the science of drawing.

The attraction of spiritual circles is not an empty phrase; the chain is perpetuated and unfolded, evolution continues even on the spiritual plane, and there are many spirits that voluntarily seek to imbibe with the radiant qualities of spirits more advanced than themselves.

Such spirits create, in the environment where they live, paintings depicting scenes of extraordinary dazzlement, of incomparable richness of color. As in architecture, these paintings are perishable at the will of the being that created them, but there are regions where, either in architecture or in painting, scenes and monuments survive after the reincarnation of their author. It is like one of the limits of space separating the etheric worlds, many worlds where life is purely spiritual and which are frequented only by very high order spirits. It is there that beings come in mission, to seek high inspirations, to initiate themselves in the cult of beauty and good by letting themselves be impregnated with radiations which have a truly divine character.

(January 20, 1922)

Literature and Eloquence

Literature and eloquence are also forms of art, powerful means of making thought shine in our world. We can say with Aesop that language is, depending on the use we make of it, what is best or what is worst. From this point of view, France has always had a privileged role. The sharpness and clarity of the French language, though poorer than others in descriptive words, has largely served the expansion of its genius and the dissemination of generous ideas. It is therefore the qualities of its language that has ensured it a distinctive place in the world and high relevance in the future.

Because of its clarity, its clear understanding of things, French has been the predestined instrument of great announcements and august revelations. Other languages have their charm, their beauty, but none succeed better in enlightening intelligences, in persuading, in convincing. Also, the elite spirits coming to Earth to fulfill a renovating mission, will preferably incarnate in francophone countries, and among them the greatest of all, so that our language can serve them as a vehicle for their high and noble thoughts throughout the world. Their presence and action, we are told from the Hereafter, will further contribute to increasing the prestige and glory of France.

French literature excels above all in the analysis of feelings and passions, it is characterized above all in the novel, whose general theme is sensual love. Under the influence of pleasurable materialism, it became bogged down with pleasure and instead of cooperating in the recovery of the nation, it contributed, more often than not, to corrupt our morals and precipitate decadence. Most writers of our time are delighted to expose their adventures in the display of spicy cynicism. From there, at times, comes the discredit of France abroad and the measures taken against our language in several education establishments. It is time for a new stream of ideas to come and inspire French art and literature with a more philosophical sense of things and a broader notion of destiny. This alone can restore to the works of thought all their scale and regenerative efficiency.

Inspired by invisible contributors and instructors, this reaction may be intensified. Writers, orators, may feel carried away by occult forces towards purer, brighter horizons. Then productions will arise on all sides, imbued with broad and elevated bodies of thought.

French thought is beginning to acquire that radiant power to which it is entitled; it will one day reach heights that music alone so far has been able to glimpse and anticipate. It will come to possess this gift of penetration, of persuasion, these aesthetic qualities which will ensure its definitive predominance. It can be seen from now on that under its influence the Latin world has been impregnated entirely with the teachings of Allan Kardec about successive lives. The works of the great initiator have been translated into all neo-Latin languages, namely, Spanish and Portuguese. Editions follow each other rapidly in Central and South America; the Spiritualist[10] idea penetrates into the most remote circles, in the form clothed by French writers.

In the last century, authors of genius had already found subjects of inspiration in psychic phenomena. One could mention Balzac, Alexandre Dumas, Théophile Gautier, Michelet, Edgard Quinet, Jean Reynaud and many others.

Romanticism, in spite of its excesses, brought to this age, like a deep wave, the notion of the divine and immortality: thus people from 1830 and 1848 had a better principled and nobler character than those of today, immersed in politics.

The romantic thrust has manifested itself as the prelude to the great movement of ideas that embraces all humanity today. From Lamartine to Victor Hugo, and Baudelaire to Gérard de Nerval, they all sought the infinite in nature and in life. The notion of successive lives is found in Lamartine's *Le Chut d'un Ange* and *Jocelyn*; then in the *Revenant*,

---

[10] [Trans. note] As seen countless times elsewhere, Léon DENIS always used the terms *Spiritualism/Spiritualist* and *Spiritism/Spiritist* interchangeably.

Les Contemplations, and *La Légende des Siècles* [*The Legend of the Ages*] of Victor Hugo; and in Baudelaire's "*La Vie Antérieure*" ["*The Former Life*"], and so on.

In more recent works, certain authors of merit, such as Paul Grendel, Elie Sauvage, Dr. Wylm, among others, have brought more developments to the psychological idea, highlighting its vast consequences. Even outside France, Rudyard Kipling and Selma Lagerlöf introduced reincarnation in their works. A whole host of young and ardent writers, not always measured, follow their example and engage in rich and fruitful ways.

The grave events of recent years[11] have everywhere created new needs for the spirit and the heart, the need to know, to believe, to discover the foci of a brighter light and more abundant sources of consolation. The collective soul of the French nation is making an effort to free itself from the embraces of materialism. Its deep Celtic intuitions wake up and carry it to those spiritual boundaries where an invisible world calls and attracts it.

The genius of France is made of balance and harmony. Despite some shortcomings in the past, it can be said that it has often served as a mediator between the most diverse schools, between the

---

[11] [Trans. note] World War I (1914–1918).

most opposite systems. Even today, in the political order, for example, France holds the middle which lies between reaction and anarchy. This was often the case during its history, in the fields of art and thought.

As we have seen, its language, which is one of the expressions of its genius, presents the qualities of precision and flexibility which make it a wonderful agent of dissemination and promotion. It knows how to lend strength and grace to ideas at the same time, and it is by this means that it can make a great contribution to initiating the world into the knowledge of higher laws.

French literature and poetry, more than all the others, have been able to reproduce all the nuances of thought and feeling; the tenderness and the energy, the charm, the infinite sweetness of an ideal; in a word, all the superhuman dreams of art and beauty. The clear genius of France is chiefly designed to unite and blend, in balanced equilibrium, the two different geniuses of the South and the North of Europe, the Latin people, and the Northern peoples. It is perhaps the meeting of these opposing elements, the ebb and flow of these diverse currents, that explains its mobility of spirit, and the sometimes unfortunate instability of its views; yet always, after a period of crisis in which the equilibrium has been altered in it, the national spirit will resume its activity and rise again.

Its mission, therefore, seems to be to provide to other peoples, somehow slower in the uptake, indications and directives from which they can draw practical and fruitful applications. It is in this sense that France is a marvelous agent of progress and human evolution, in its concern for truth and light, and for the beauty of the forms with which it takes pleasure in clothing them with.

Such qualities have assigned it a preponderant role in the dissemination of philosophical and moral Spiritism, whereas the Anglo-Saxon countries have endeavored to represent it especially in its scientific and experimental aspects.

After moments of trial and error and obscurity, the genius of France, which is none other than the still living and immortal soul of Gaul, is rising again, and, with a vigorous effort, emerging from the earthly quagmires in order to rush into the sky and discover new horizons, new perspectives in the future, showing them as a goal to humanity on the move.

For all those who know how to study and understand the genius of France, under the skepticism that sometimes covers it, the Celtic soul reappears, and at solemn times, it is its impulses that determine virile resolutions and the decisive acts.

It is this Celtic soul that inspired Joan of Arc, and by her hands has delivered France from the yoke of the English. It also has caused this powerful spiritualistic explosion which, in the revolutionary epoch, brought to all the essential notion of freedom, thus assuring the triumph of the modern soul over the depressing theories of determinism and fatalism. It is always this soul that, in the dark days of the year 1914, awakened all the living forces of the nation and raised it, heroically and sublimely, in the face of German despotism and Teutonic militarism. More recently, it opposed like a dike the red wave of Bolshevism.

In this respect, France has greater duties than other nations, because it has received greater gifts, more brilliant qualities. Also its responsibilities are heavier and more extensive. Today, a task higher than all others is emerging for it around the world. It is a matter of introducing humans to the beauties of a wider future, richer than that which philosophical and religious conceptions have been able to envisage. It is a matter of guiding the human ascent to the majestic peaks of the idea, where the fires of a new day are ignited, the dawn of a nobler and more dignified civilization, free from the plagues that have hindered until now the harsh and painful way of humanity.

Other nations each have their important task, but France surpasses them all by the variety of its aptitudes and activities. That is why the whole world has its eyes fixed on it, waiting for the sign that will trace its new evolution. O, living soul of France, free yourself from the heavy materialistic influences that still oppress you, rise to the noble ideal which is your mission to acquire and spread all over the world. Only when the new revelation is known to all peoples, giving expression to the superb form of your genius, will humans understand their great destiny, as well as the duties and burdens it imposes on them. Justice and peace will finally reign over the regenerated Earth, and through that your role will be visible to everyone. You will be revered by generations, and your glory will be illuminated with a brilliance that nothing can tarnish anymore![12]

In eloquence, the movement of thought is represented not only by the word, but also by the gesture that emphasizes and accentuates its effects. In this, more than in any other matter, a just measure is necessary, because any excess as well as the absence of gesturing, should be carefully avoided.

The majority of great speakers are touched by the breath of the invisible. The inspiration descends into them in a rushing stream, and brings out the expressions, the forms, the images that stir the enthusiasm of the crowds. At times, they feel lifted up and carried away by an irresistible current. During my career as a lecturer, I have often felt the sensation of a powerful occult help and I knew its cause. The spirit of Jerome of Prague,[13] my protector, my guide, has always assisted me in my task as a disseminator. Sometimes, when appearing before a large audience, often indifferent or even

---

[12] [Trans. note] These personal assumptions show the author's unbridled love and admiration for his homeland at the time, tempered by history later on.

[13] Jerome of Prague (c. 1365–1416) was a Czech philosopher and theologian.

hostile, while speaking, I was plagued by physical discomfort, a violent migraine that paralyzed my thought and my action. But then, responding to my ardent call, to my prayer, my spirit guide intervened. By an energetic magnetization, it reestablished my organic balance and restored my lucidity, my means of action. At other times, after contradictory debates lasting several hours, after oral struggles with fierce opponents, whether materialists or religious figures, despite my exhaustion, I still found accents, vibrating intonations which astonished and stirred the audience. One day I had the understanding of this phenomenon, seeing it renew itself before my eyes.

It was in Aix-les-Bains, France, in the parish church, during a religious solemnity in honor of Joan of Arc. In presence of Cardinal Dubillard and a compact crowd, a young priest ascended the pulpit to pronounce the panegyric of the heroine. A medium from Lyon, Mrs. Forget, who was sitting at my side, suddenly said to me: "I can see the spirit of Jerome, it is standing in the pulpit, behind the priest." I became attentive to what was going to happen. The young priest began in a calm tone, his harmonious phrases unfolding methodically, then, little by little, the tone rose, the voice became vibrant and, at last, powerful accents, which I recognized, made the vaults of the building resound. This was an example of what had happened to myself in many cases.

This sort of inspired eloquence, I have been able to find it in certain mediums, albeit very rarely.

There are some who "incorporate" in the same seance several spirits, whose discourses reveal very distinct personalities of great originality, and which cannot be confused with each other, or with that of the medium.

The most remarkable subject that I met during my travels was the daughter of a teacher at the Lycée de Marseille in France. In a state of trance, she served not only as a transmission organ for discarnate spirit speakers, but also for other extraordinary entities, as for example the famous Mrs. Geoffrin, whose delicacy of mind, finesse and the penetrating charm of her manners, together with a rather old-fashioned language, did not leave any room for doubt or suspicion of simulation.

This is how influences from above are felt in a thousand ways, and that the proof of the survival and solidarity which connects the world of the living with the world of the dead is becoming more and more consolidated.

The real merit, whether of the writer or the speaker, is to make people think, to instill in souls the noble and holy enthusiasms, to raise them to the radiant heights where they perceive the vibrations of divine thought, in supreme communion.

But in order for the soul to expand and blossom in the exhilaration of higher joys, it is good that harmony should be added to speech and style: music must come to open up to intelligence paths that may lead to the understanding of divine laws, and the possession of eternal beauty.

The influence of music is immense and takes the most diverse forms, depending on each individual. The deep, rich bass sounds act on us in such a way that the best in us is externalized. The soul emerges and refers back to the living sources of inspiration.

It has happened to me more than once, that when I had to give a lecture in a big city, I would direct myself the night before to some lyric theater. There, hidden deep in a theater box, completely isolated, I lost interest in all that was happening in the concert hall or on the stage, to let myself be lulled by the music. Under the combined action of instruments and voices, a flood of ideas rose to my brain, thoughts and images arising in full bloom from the depths of the self. And at these moments I built my subject with a wealth of materials, a profusion of arguments, an abundance of forms and expressions that I could not have found in silence, and which were not always timely represented in my memory.

Hearing big church organs and sacred songs can produce even higher impressions in me. During the moments when I can hear good music, the power of art opens for me a domain of hidden treasures, of the most beautiful psychic faculties, then let me fall heavily back again into the habitual current of thought and everyday life.

On Earth, it is through thought, written or oral, that faith is communicated and taught by humans. But in the spiritual world, so say our guides, music is the sublime expression of divine thought.

Already here below one can notice that a writer or an orator who studies harmony, proportionately increases the resources of his or her imagination, penetration of things, and facility of expressing them. Have not some individuals of genius declared that their most beautiful works were conceived at hours of ecstasy, induced by the hearing of the distant echoes of some distant echoes of celestial concerts, that is to say, of the infinite orchestra of the worlds?

Lessons of the Esthete

VII

This evening I am going to discuss the artistic field that has thought as its pure vehicle, that is, thought in literature and in eloquence. In our last talk, I have shown how, from an artistic point of view, the reflection of thought could, thanks to wonderfully subtle environments, be attached to fluidic molecules and, through various shades representing ideas, constitute paintings, in which the art of color reproduces scenes of beauty, as symbols. This was said in transitional manner. Now, what would be the play of thought in art?

Thinking is above all a gift of observation. The human being, incarnate or discarnate, can explore every environment in thought. I will leave out beings that are essentially material in character, and that carry their thoughts in environments where the avidity of lucre or lust reigns.

But, among evolved beings, thought rises much higher. You know that, on Earth, this thought is attached to the painting of customs and habits, to the analysis of characters, and that it is also translated into writings taking more or less symbolic forms. In the spiritual world, thought naturally becomes much freer; it possesses in itself the exact reflection of all the sentiments which may have been imprinted upon it in the past, impressing it at various degrees. The spirit, when freed from matter, and after having reached a certain elevation, can transmit its thought directly to beings still incarnated. Hence the phenomenon of inspiration.

Take, for example, a highly evolved spiritual being that professes the cult of perfect beauty. It will recognize on Earth human beings whose thoughts are already reflected in shining lights. It will feel attracted to them and its own thought will mingle with theirs; its fluidic molecules will intensely vivify the material, generative molecules springing from the brain of the being that is living on Earth.

Spirit writers spirits will approach the artisans of the pen; ancient speakers will feel attracted to the masters of the word. This is what happens for the transmission from the spiritual plane to the world.

Now, in an evolved being, the desire to radiate its thought through space is no lesser than that which draws it to the inhabited worlds. Let us take a great earthly thinker: back in the spirit world, this individual will reveal to the spirits that surround it the essence of its acquired virtues. Then, reading in the brains of incarnate beings, it will project waves impregnated with all the qualities of its thought.

It is an imperishable work carried out by this transmission through fluidic bodies, because, when the beam of thought is intense, it impresses the brains so that they always bear the imprint of the impression felt.

Thinkers of the Earth and those of the spiritual plane are closely correlated. Some spirits spend their existence in the Hereafter collecting these impressions. When, in turn, they feel able to share it with less advanced beings, they go down again to incarnate and become those great writers, great poets, and illustrious persons who earn the admiration of those around them.

The art of eloquence is formed in the same way, but more subtly. In the speaker, the vibrations of the spiritual world are strongly felt through the body, as a result of a more intense work done before birth and by the action of a much stronger will. Each speaker, to varying degrees, possesses the gift of intuition, in a more or less developed degree. In general, the qualities of a master of eloquence result from a preparation made on the spiritual plane, *thanks to the sum of the impressions felt in that environment.*

According to the arrangement of material molecules, art, in the person of letters or in the orator, will be more or less pure. You have proof of this by analyzing the different classes of writers, poets, and orators. In the ordinary writer, thought is still charged with a materialism that is often heavy. In the poet, the ideal and the symbol pierce deeper and are all the more admirable as they are purer. It is the same with the speaker; you have evidence of this in the contrast offered by the low-level orator with the one who, profane or sacred, devotes his or her physical organ to the defense and popularization of maxims and precepts almost all emanating from the Most High.

Modes of exteriorizing thought are as multiple as there are individuals. The categories of thinkers can be distinguished on the spiritual plane by the luminous intensity which emerges from each fluidic being. Your word, of an absolutely material nature, is something unknown there; also, when a being returns to the spirit realm, it must submit itself to a new adaptation and its language must become that of the interpretation of colors. There is in color a range so subtle and varied that the smallest modulations can represent the slightest fluctuations of thought.

An art-loving person will be able to receive and transmit thoughts of infinite delicacy, and I assure you that, in my opinion, the art of thought is closer to God than any other art.

What delights we have on the spiritual plane when we feel the vibrations of a being with a character of remarkable purity and elevation, resulting in radiations of a hue wonderfully rich in fluidic atoms.

I will not repeat here an analysis of all the domains of thought. I simply wanted to give you the mechanism of the transfer of art from Earth to the spiritual plane and its fundamental role in the middle of the fluidic layers. I will add, and I insist to say to you, that thought is the easiest thing for us to transmit, because we take real joy in helping the moral illumination of the beings which surround you.

Your human brains, closed to the sublime ideas emanating from the Divine Being, cannot currently understand the sequence of forces in action in the universe. Suffice it to know that God's mind reaches everyone and everything, that none of its radiation is lost, and that we, poor dragonflies, have the duty to transmit the best of ourselves to those who can understand us. This is where art comes in our aid. So stick to thinking with art. Love those who think well. For, you can remain sure that, the very essence of this thought is a reflection of life on the spiritual plane; so, be sorry for to those who do not know how to think. Art is one of the forms of beauty, and, like thought, it must be its vehicle, for *beauty contains in itself the principles of goodness, greatness, and justice.*

(January 27, 1922)

VIII

Today I would like to talk about the transmission of art on Earth, in order to show you the part taken in artistic compositions by the spirits that continue a work whose elements draw on fluidic sources and spread through material means. We have seen how, in the spiritual world, an evolved being could, by means of reflections, reproduce amid its artistic qualities, subjects borrowed from the domain of architecture, painting, sculpture or thought.

If you remember well, it is thanks to the faculty possessed by each fluidic being that enable them to reconstitute the elements and the scenes of their successive lives, that they have learned and retained all things that form their divine universality. Now I would like to talk about, while leaving the subject of intuition aside, the reincarnated spirit that on Earth, for example, when its bodily development is sufficient, will be able to vibrate in its being the fluidic molecules impregnated with radiation, resulting from many lives on the spiritual plane. These can be translated on your planet as the so-called native gifts, which will bring the living being to a distinguished situation as an artist or thinker.

Let's take an architect, for example: After having gathered the elements of the drawing which will furnish its brain with materials capable of concentrating the radiations, these, intuitively, will lead the human being to create ideal forms, inspired even unknowingly by images and settings which can be reconstituted by the radiation attached to its brain atoms.

Depending on the number of lifetimes experienced, according to one's will to study them, to understand them, these atoms will be more or less animated with a life of their own; and also according to the flexibility of harmony of the lines which will serve as their conductor, the work thus created will be more or less rich and lofty.

On the one hand, there is mechanical work, external work, that is taught during the tangible lifetime of a being; on the other hand, a fixation of radiating molecules, impregnated with previous knowledge. On these lines more or less flexible and malleable, a production is realized, a creation of an object. The architect at his or her table, suddenly sees lines and vaults appear, a monument is built in accordance with his or her will. It is the molecules that, according to the acquired geometric knowledge, act by extension on the brain lobes of the artist, concretizing images idealized in the abstract.

I used the example of the architect because, in your view, architectural art is the most tangible art. On the spiritual world, the mind travels through infinite worlds; there the art of the line is the first letter of a grandiose alphabet that I will call the **wide range of forms, sounds and colors.** *A living being will draw from the spiritual plane and from different worlds all necessary forms, which will then be reproduced in sculpture. For a more subtle spirit, occupying a higher level of art, painting will be preferred, since the relief for the painter is only fluidic and must be reproduced by the brush.*

The third step is the one that gives access to thinkers, philosophers, and writers. The geometric works, of which I have spoken, become almost fictional; the geometry of thought being simply an increasingly subtle analysis of beings and things.

In the next talk, I will discuss music and I attempt to show you how musical inflections should and can synthesize all the arts, since they are the vehicle of the breath that creates and animates everyone and everything.

In my earthly life, I touched all the arts: painting, sculpture, music. Now God has allowed me to live in spheres where everything is vibration, and I would like to give you a glimpse of this heavenly life.

(February 3, 1922)

Theater
and
Music

In the previous chapter, we have seen that the preponderance of French literature has long been asserted. It possessed everything that seduced and captivated. But evolution is necessary; a time comes, in the history of thought, where speech and gesture are no longer sufficient to translate the emotions of the soul. It is then that the musical sense awakens and comes into play in literature itself, which should be a reflection of the higher harmony. The manifestation of this tendency marks one more step in the ascension of the spirit toward the summits, as it happens on the spiritual plane, where speech ceases to be used.

This evolution of thought and its manifestations, in their multiple forms – the arts, sciences, literature – will be brought about by an increasingly closer and deeper cooperation of the spirit world with the human work.

The Spiritist revelation provides us with inexhaustible subjects of inspiration and feeling. It introduces us to the conditions of a more subtle life, a life which is the essential objective of all ascension and whose details bring into our programs of studies and research a variety of elements which expand to infinity the limits of our conceptions, of our knowledge. This inevitably results in a fertilization, a complete renewal of the ideal that faded away and deteriorated under the influence of materialistic or dogmatic theories, whose empire will eventually end, despite the desperate efforts of its supporters.

Therefore Spiritism gives thought a new vigorous impulsion. It traces an immense circle around the history of beings and worlds, which allows for all sorts of dreams, all sort of flights of imagination. It unfolds new issues about everything that makes the power, the grandeur, the beauty of the universe.

So far, literary form may have seemed enough to exalt national sentiments and all that pertains to the epic of the human race, and to planetary life in general. It may even seemed to be excellent and produced masterpieces that will remain as imperishable monuments of thought and feeling. But, no matter its excellence, literature becomes poor when it comes to reproducing the higher forms of human activity.

As humanity's horizons widen and it communicates with universal life, more perfect forms of expression and feeling become necessary in order to respond to the vibratory state, to the increasing radiations of the soul. A sure intuition, the instinct of beauty, leads the spiritual being to substitute in the expression of its thought and the impulses of its soul the pure harmony with the word and the letter. The revelations of the unseen incite the soul to employ in turn the processes used in the spirit realm.

True literary merit, the qualities of a beautiful style, consist in provoking thought and reflections in the reader, in creating a mental atmosphere which encourage the development and enrichment of the reader's faculties and moral powers.

There is no doubt that making one think is noble, but what is even more noble and meritorious is to elevate the soul to the heights where all its faculties may flourish in light and love. It is to help it reach the degree of evolution which will allow it to taste, no longer with its material organs, but with its inner deep senses, the joys and gratifications of the higher life; to feel this supreme vibration which fills the universe, in line with God, the great Esthete, and which induces definitive communion with divine thought, the ecstasy of Beauty when understood and realized.

Really beautiful and strong works of art have become a rarity in modern times, whether in literature or even in the theater. This latter could be a powerful means of intellectual and moral education, by the elevation of thoughts and feelings, and by noble examples put before the public eye.

But instead of its magnificent and beneficent mission, the theater has too often become just a means of flattering unhealthy passions and exciting the senses. In all these cases it has become the work of skeptical sensualists, ignorant or reckless when it comes to the true purpose of life. This is a glittering and unhealthy scum, the morbid fruit of a civilization debased by the lure of pleasure and riches.

How often, attracted by the title of a new play, by a glittering new poster, I went to the greatest Parisian theaters, in the hope of finding there some substantial spiritual food in the course of a well spent evening. Alas, my disappointments can no longer be counted! Instead of the fertile substance I was expecting, there were only banal or equivocal scenes unfolding under my eyes. Sure, a lot of wit had probably gone into it. Clever words shone in sparkling exchanges or floated like soap bubbles in the spotlight; yet the slightest breath carried away without leaving any trace in the memory or consciousness of the spectator, for elevated thoughts, encouraging examples, and comforting teaching were nowhere to be found. So, the impression that emanated from it was one of emptiness or impotence, if not something worse.

The dignity of the theater must be restored to the stage, thus reconstituting the ideal that has been degraded by inadequate and corrupt authors.

In the changing spectacle of customs, habits and social circles which constitute the fabric of comedy, we must know how to choose what can elevate minds and hearts. But with our contemporary authors it is always the theme of guilty love, of unhealthy love, that dominates; and thus, by sharpening our carnal appetites and feeding passions, it precipitates the decadence of the theater in the work of general corruption.

It seems that our era has a special inclination for being poisoned. Materially speaking, this taste for poison is translated as an excessive use of alcohol and tobacco, or even opium, ether and other harmful drugs, all causing physical disorders, ruining your health, eroding the human race. Intellectually speaking, this taste manifests itself in a sort of predilection for popular literature and spectacles. Here the evil is still more serious, because it is in the conscience, the moral sense, and the dignity of the affected human being. And from this results an overflow of sensual appetites, a defective orientation for life and our faculties.

That is why it is necessary to look for all means of elevating souls and thoughts toward those regions from which the breath from above sweep away all impurities.

From these radiant summits, we contemplate and penetrate better the essence of things and come down with the amount of energy necessary to continue the struggles of this world and to remove from ourselves any unhealthy temptations or degrading pleasures.

Poetry is essentially only a form of music. It is subject to the same laws of rhythm and vibration, which are the laws of life in its higher states.

Antiquity, which created the genre, understood it. The ancient poet was both a singer and a musician. Nowadays, however, poetry is just one of the forms of literature. Like all art manifestations in general, it has lost its august character and fell into banality. We are inundated with a flood of verses without elevation and without beauty.

But verse cannot stand mediocrity. And that is why, in the Middle Ages as nowadays, writers of genius such as Dante, Lamartine, Victor Hugo and others have been able to preserve poetry's brilliance and character of greatness, thus saving it from an irreversible fall. To express the sublime ideal, all words are powerless. Having reached a certain height, thought finds only human terms, appropriate to the requirements of our lower plane, but unable to translate the impressions of higher life. And that is what the Esthete deplores. As soon as the insufficiency of human language is revealed, music, with its infinite resources, becomes the only form that can adapt itself to the eternal beauty of the universe, the only way to express the sensations of a delighted soul, merging with divine thought.

Speech, when united with music, can provide the thinker with an intense, even more penetrating expression. Yet, nowadays, the application of this mode has sometimes become really vulgar. Ballads and songs had, until recently, their charm and their flavor. Today, under the influence of certain public circles, they are nothing more than a profanation, a debasement of the original idea.

Still, despite impure cloaks that sacrilegious hands have mired, music rises to radiant heights of thought and poetry, and becomes capable of translating the noblest sentiments. This is its own true element. There, everything is waves, vibrations, harmonies, light. That is why poetry, to remain in its true role, must be inspired by the laws of musical harmony and reproduce them with fidelity.

We know that music plays a big role in prophetic and religious inspiration. It sets rhythm in fluidic emissions and facilitates the action of high spirits. That is why it has its place in Spiritist meetings, in seances which participants are advised precede with a hymn appropriate to the circumstances. Often spirit guides engage participants in singing a song to facilitate the events. But, up to now, it should be noted that Spiritists have found themselves very destitute and forced to resort to common songs, banalities unworthy of the aim pursued. It is not without a painful impression that I have witnessed more than once the lack of musical resources used in groups. That is why I myself composed a hymn dedicated to "The Unseen," whose music was due to a lady with a certain aesthetic sense and goodwill. But here is Mr. A. E., a well-known composer, who has just obtained from the spirit of Beethoven, through a medium, a Spiritist canticle worthy of the composer, which will hopefully see the light of day.[14] Spiritists will thus finally have a musical invocation harmonized with their thoughts and aspirations.

Regarding any work of literature, poetry, or art, the choice of means must be appropriate to the greatness intended.

In reality, poetry is everywhere where we know how to place it. It does not express itself only through verses; it can permeate all forms of written or spoken language, all aspects of art. Poetry is the expression of beauty spread throughout the universe. It is the communicative warmth of the soul that has grasped and understood the profound meaning of things, the law of the supreme harmonies, and which then seeks to penetrate other souls by the means which belong to itself.

All beings are sensitive to music. Even animals cannot escape its influence. We all know the legend of Orpheus who could, by the sound of his lyre,

---

[14] [Trans. note] Such hymn remains little know to this day.

draw the beasts of the forest after him. Insects themselves can feel musical vibrations. When I go to the piano, honeybees flutter around me in a particular fashion.

The power of music is also demonstrated by the influence of a song on people. Music is the companion at work, a support in patient and repeated efforts, and joy of any home, because it exalts the forces and the feelings of the human being. A song can also be a means of elevation, but, as we have seen, nowadays it is too often dragged into mudflats, thus losing all its refreshing character.

The last two lessons of the Esthete, which we will find further in this chapter, take us back to the serene heights of Art. They end the series of communications that my group has received from this great spirit, whose identity we now know.

When incarnated, he was one of the most eminent artists of the Italian Renaissance,[15] at once an architect, painter and sculptor. Music was not foreign to this spirit either. Today, it lives in the higher spheres where Beauty and Good reign supreme, and where it pursues the realization of magnificent conceptions. Our guides tell us that we must consider its participation in our mediumistic work as a unique favor, so I wish to express our gratitude to it, as well as to the sovereign Power that has allowed such an intervention.

Next, I will be talking about music and include lessons given by the spirit of Massenet, more

---
[15] [Trans. note] Most likely Michelangelo (1475–1564).

specifically devoted to this great art. Thanks to them a ray of celestial life has penetrated our darkness, giving more breadth and depth to my feeble human essays.

LESSONS OF THE ESTHETE

IX

Today I will talk about the music of the spiritual plane considered as a means of transmitting artistic thought. I know another spirit, which is closer to you, that has already tried to make you understand how the waves, which you call musical, are created, then transmitted through space, to end up in different worlds. It has already been told to you that these so-called sonorities to you are like tints to us, which, transported on fluidic molecules, roam the vibratory fields and communicate to beings impressions comparable to those which your ears perceive when you hear a range of harmonized sounds on this or that degree of vibration.

When a note is struck on Earth, if it emanates from the major scale, it will send you a feeling full joy. If it is from the minor scale, on the contrary, your brain will feel a sensation made of depth, sometimes sadness or great pain, following the modulation of the chords and the number of notes put into play.

Therefore to these two great principles, namely, major and minor, correspond two sensations, joy and pain. Between these notes, you have an infinity of combinations which, by this very fact, will form images. Like the sculptor forms a virtual image, a group of notes and chords, whether modulated in major or minor, will form by their style a series of thoughts, which become more or less comprehensible depending on the evolution of the modes of music.

So here we have an established point: the visual arts form images and the art of musical waves also forms images, but more subtle ones, whose content is more fragile, and whose understanding is more delicate. According to the degree of evolution of beings, this understanding will be more or less profound. That is why often, on your globe, an individual of medium culture will be impressed, whereas his or her brain will remain refractory when it comes to borrow from the alphabet to express their thoughts by means of waves that you describe as musical.

On the spiritual plane, as you know, there are no musical instruments, it is our spiritual perceptions that receive the transmitting waves of musical thought. It will therefore be necessary to directly impregnate the beings who must receive waves of this nature. As for other artists, the spirit with the musical sense evolved, being able to feel infinitely sweet and subtle sensations, can also transmit them using your instruments and through the brain of one of your performers.

In order to be set in motion by fluidic waves, matter requires an intermediate agent, which is your brain, that in this case acts as an attracting pole and a sensitive plate, from which all the radiations emanate from the fluids.

Great musicians on Earth may, like other artists, receive inspiration either from the spiritual plane or as a result of some previous works. This is exactly the same phenomenon that occurs among other artists.

On the spiritual plane, our means are much faster than yours; we do not need an instrument to exchange our thoughts, and our music is all impressions, acting directly on the most sensitive part of our fluidic being, that which contains the divine spark in different degrees, and which, in you, is represented by the heart organ.

The other arts are reflected by sculptural and pictorial images, which are modes of transmission of thought and replace speech for us. Music is a special impression, which invades the fluidic being entirely, plunging it into ecstasy, bliss, making it feel sensations of joy, quietude, fulfillment, anxiety, sorrow, pain, regret, or remorse. This encompasses, roughly speaking, the whole gamut of ascending and descending sensations, ranging from pink to black; black being nothingness.

From this point of view, from a purely artistic point of view, you can imagine the infinite number of sensations that can affect an already evolved spirit. Already on Earth, you can prepare to receive these sensations in the Hereafter, by removing from you any material or sensual satisfaction. Look for artistic attractions, however poor they may be; enrich your thought, give your nerves a nourishment of warm vibrations; populate your brain with sensations that translate in you as analytical studies of your earthly lifetimes. All this will one day reverberate on the spiritual plane a hundredfold, because the vibrations stored in your carnal being will wake up and call, like a lyre with a thousand strings, the attractive sensations that can engender the most harmonious, highest feelings, which circulate on the currents emanating directly from the divine sphere.

This should be the **pinnacle** *of art, an infinite artistic sensation.*

Poor earthly humans cannot feel the ineffable joys that fill us when these sensations come to touch our ecstatic spirits.

What would these sensations be? I will try as a conclusion to tell you, with God's permission, what they can be. It will not be easy because it would open to you a direct view of the divine work. Your spirit guides will pray. I hope to give you, in a few words, an idea of this great work of beauty, light and harmony.

(February 10, 1922)

X

The final subject of our talks is rather more delicate, and the resources I find in this medium are so limited that I must ask you to excuse the poverty of the expressions used. We will be almost entering and hovering in the divine realm.

Today, I would like to be able to open a window into this celestial azure, which is home to all radiations and should summarize all virtues for you, all the intellectual and moral powers.

You have found in your human lifetimes that each being possesses, to varying degrees, either by intuition or as a result of its own will, the qualities it has acquired on your globe, in previous lives or through aspirations toward divine fluidic spheres.

I come to tell you that the Divine Being is a radiant core, composed of all things and composing all things.

Your earthly imaginations cannot grasp that. It is not necessary anyway, because on your plane, you must not rise higher than evolution allows you. But from the spiritual plane we have a stronger feeling that there is a sphere, a field of action in which the fluidic waves impress and vibrate in us the spiritual beings, in you the bodily beings; and which represents the power, the beauty, the harmony of the divine. This harmony is the very essence of art: it is this which, when dispensed appropriately, makes the brains of geniuses vibrate and sets into action intelligent beings in the process of evolution, through reasoned and sustained work and volition. These spheres open up access to the divine field. We can picture this latter better than you, but, notwithstanding we cannot yet blend in with it.

I would like to open wide the window to communicate to you the divine thought, to tell you in what way and by what integral fluidic radiation the creative work continues, but it is not in my power to open completely the door to this azure creator. It is only through a very small opening that I can communicate to your brains and your hearts the little I know myself.

The divine core is therefore in constant and regular action, creating the universal motion. It is through it that God's creatures are born, live and transform themselves, according to the purity of the physical elements employed. The divine radiance is more or less felt on the molecules that imprison their minds.

The human body can be more or less perfect. There is the question of atavism and of spiritual attraction in the more or less pure circles that the bodies pass through. The creations from the divine field are of a magnificent elevation. As one gets closer to it, one can better understand the functioning of this great organism that is the Universe.

A constant fact is that, when cogs are persistently moving, they get rusty, thus preventing their axes from moving regularly. Rust is manifested in organized beings as a grip exerted by faults in lower order environments; so, when there is a crack, defects and vices may crop up.

This is how good degenerates. It can revive itself in contact with pure sources, like a worker in precision mechanics can put back on its pivots an instrument that no longer works.

Through an always sustained volition, through a direct appeal, you should aspire to the vivifying rays, by which you will be able to keep in touch with the fluidic beams which emanate from the divine field and which will revive, by their action, the parts of your being soiled by the rust of faults and vices.

It is through these relations, almost constant with these fluidic beams, that all beings, on this world or on the spiritual plane, retain their aptitudes, means of elevation, and intuitions which form the generic meaning of the word art.

This is why each being must be concerned about its progress and keep in itself this attracting pole which, translating virtually in capacities corresponding to the being's desires, will be more or less enamored of art. This almost magical word, art, means: rays emanating from a supra-cosmic field; this ray maintains with us the light, the magnificence, the power, the beauty, the goodness emanating from the core which forms the center of the divine fluidic field.

In a preceding talk, I mentioned this most sensitive spot of the human organism called heart. It is from the heart that the vibration starts, spreading through your whole being, providing it with the means to exteriorize noble and elevated thoughts. But, this vibration, analyze it well, return within yourselves; and you will understand that when a generous feeling makes your heart vibrate, it is that it received at the same moment the impulsion, by a wave emanating from the divine, of a noble and generous feeling.

It is thanks to a rational evolution on different planes, in different worlds, that beings are gradually becoming purified. What is being done around you will be bigger around beings, worlds, and spheres.

To conclude, art is for the human being the call from the divine field. The more a being by its will and its actions approaches God, the more apt it becomes to feel the divine waves and vibrations. Depending on its degree of evolution, such vibrations will be translated into creations of virtues. The word virtue being used here in a very general sense. In my spirit, it means everything that is worthy of being loved. Art is therefore one of the means to feel the greatness of God. We must thank the Creator for always allowing us to be in touch with it. It is up to us to know how to make ourselves more and more worthy of it. Art must be revered and loved, since through immensity it is it that functions as the messenger of the immortal radiance and universal divine motion.

Let us keep in the depths of our selves this sensitive spot which is for us one of the poles of communication with our Creator. Whether we are equipped with a carnal body or a spiritual envelope, the divine ray always comes to us, when we do not leave inactive, by guilty inertia, this machine which must serve as a transmitter of fluids and divine waves. The evolved being has the joy of helping to perfect and preserve beings which are more material than itself.

Art, messenger of the divine, is a torch that should never be extinguished. It should make us understand that God's beauty and glory are infinite. There can be art even in the smallest actions if, by adapting itself to the environment in which it is acting, the divine ray which exteriorizes itself spreads around it a shower of beneficial waves.

As there is evolution in beings, there is evolution in the arts. You have the primitives in the arts, as well as in actions and virtues, but always the same spark shines in conditions where it can manifest itself, to affirm the greatness of God.

(February 11, 1922)

EARTHLY VERSUS SPIRITUAL MUSIC

Music is the voice of deep heavens. Everything on the spiritual plane is translated into harmonic vibrations, and certain classes of spirits communicate with each other only by means of sound waves.

On Earth, the symphony and the melody are only weakened and distorted echoes of celestial concerts. Our most perfect instruments always have something mechanical and hard, whereas the processes of emission of the spiritual plane produce sounds of infinite delicacy.

That is why at every step of the ladder of worlds, and in the hierarchy of spirits, music occupies a considerable place in the manifestations of worship rendered by souls to God. In the higher spheres, it becomes one of the usual forms of a being's life, which feels immersed in waves of harmony of inexpressible intensity and sweetness.

At the great celebrations in the spiritual world – so say our spirit guides – when souls gather by the millions to pay homage to the Creator in the radiance of their faith and their love, emanations escape from them, luminous radiations which are colored with blended hues and which change into melodious vibrations. The colors are transformed into sounds, and from this communion of fluids, thoughts and feelings emerges a sublime symphony, to which correspond the distant chords from the spheres, the innumerable stars which populate the immensity.

Then from above, other more powerful accents descend and a universal hymn send shivers down heaven and earth. At these perceived accents, the spirit expands and flourishes, feels itself to live in divine communion, and enters into a rapture close to ecstasy.

On Earth, the symphony is the most winged form of music. When it is chained to words, it looks like a Wingless Victory, which crawled without being able to take off or glide from above. Word-related music loses some of its prestige and magnitude. Yet the melody lulls us, charms us, enchants us; it engraves in our memory the motives we like to repeat and which comfort us for the sadness of each day. Yet this music seems very poor if we compare it to the harmonies of the spiritual plane. To understand and taste these latter, one must have fairly developed psychical senses.

We have seen more than once in seances, big tears rolling on the cheeks of certain mediums, who could hear the echoes of the eternal symphony. The medium G. Aubert, though utterly ignorant of music, when in a complete state of automatism, would play on the piano, sonatas, original and varied tunes, in which we recognized the workmanship of Beethoven, Bach, Chopin, and Berlioz, among others. Most famous composers have themselves testified to hearing voices and sounds that do not come from Earth, in their hours of retreat.[16]

During the celebrated sittings held by Jesse Shepard,[17] a Scottish medium, in all the great capitals and doing the tour of several sovereign courts in Europe, as well as in the seances of Dr. Sant'Angelo, in Rome, celestial choruses and chords of many invisible instruments were heard. Solo arias made it possible to recognize the voices of famous deceased singers.

Mme. de Koning-Nierstrasz recounts one of these seances in the following terms:[18] "J. Shepard stayed at my house in The Hague [Holland] for about six weeks. One evening, a few friends and I were

---

[16] See Léon DENIS, *Into the Unseen* (New York: USSF, 2017), ch. XIV, "Psychical sight and hearing in the waking state."

[17] [Trans. note] Later known as Francis Grierson. His full name was Benjamin Henry Jesse Francis Grierson Shepard.

[18] *Revue Scientifique et Morale du Spiritisme*, Paris, October 1921, p. 303.

together. The medium having risen half entranced, went to the piano. Rappings struck on all sides, lights fluttered about the room like butterflies ... Suddenly voices of men and women filled the air. It was a choir singing a sort of hymn, the Hosanna and Glory to the Father were heard by all of us. Sometimes it was a choir, sometimes women's voices, with a soprano dominating all the singing. Sitting next to the medium, I noticed that he had never opened his mouth. Two days later, one of my neighbors said to me: 'Ah! Madam, I enjoyed the beautiful concert you had the other night at home, what musicians, and what a beautiful chorale they performed!' Then I asked her:"

"Madam, did you hear one voice at a time or a whole choir?"

"'A choir,' replied the lady, 'though I could distinctly hear the soprano. Tell me, who was singing so marvelously?'"

"This spontaneous testimony put to rest any hypothesis of hallucination."

Regarding the music of the spirits, we read in the introductory "Biography" found in *Spirit Teachings* (London: Spiritualist Alliance, 1898) of William Stainton Moses, a professor at Oxford University (UK), the description of phenomena obtained in a room devoid of piano, violin or any other musical instrument.

"We had a sound of which it is exceedingly difficult to offer an adequate description. The best idea of it I can give is to ask the reader to imagine the soft tone of a clarinet gradually increasing in intensity until it rivaled the sound of a trumpet, and then, by degrees, diminishing to the original subdued note of the clarinet until it eventually died away in a long drawn-out melancholy wail ... It is a noteworthy fact that in no case did the controlling agencies produce more than single notes or at best isolated passages. This they accounted for as due to the peculiarly unmusical organization of the medium."

On the other hand, one reads in the British journal *Light* of April 30, 1921, all of the following stories, which show another type of these manifestations, obtained at the bedside of the dying and perceived by other witnesses.

"Many books might be filled with accounts of visions of the dying and supernormal happenings at the time of death. We have listened to several such accounts, some of them from persons who had no bias in favor of Spiritualism; who would, in fact, have been shocked by having their experiences recounted under such a head! But we have found especial interest in cases of music heard at the bedside of dying persons. Amongst classical examples might be cited that of the little captive Louis XVII, who died in the Temple after the execution of his father, Louis XVI, in the French Revolution. Beauchesne tells how the child, shortly before his death, when asked whether he was in pain, replied, 'Oh yes, but not so much. The music is so beautiful!' Several questions were asked about the music, but the child persisted that he could hear it. It came 'from above,' and he was astonished that no one else heard it."

"Then there is the well-known instance of Jacob Boehme and the sweet music which accompanied his departure from earth. In this instance also no one but he could hear it."

"It was different in the case of Goethe's death when the music was heard by others who were at the bedside of the dying poet."

From all parts of the United Kingdom we hear stories of those harmonies from Above, heard by the dying, and often by those who assisted them.

"Mrs. Leaning sends us the following cases:"

"When Lily Sewell was dying music was heard apparently coming from a corner of the room, on two days preceding the death. This was not audible to the child herself, but was heard by both parents in the room, another daughter in the passage, and a servant at work two floors below. On the third day, that on which the child died, the sound was like that of an Aeolian harp, seeming to pass through the room and house, and out of the door."

"A Master at Eton, in 1881, attending on his mother's death-bed, heard within a few minutes after the passing, the low, soft music as of three girls' voices singing a hymn, recognized as *The strife is o'er*, etc., which was audible to two others present, and to the doctor in attendance, who looked out of the window to discover the singers ..."

Then the story of the death of Dr. Kenealy's younger brother is thus told: "His brother's bedroom opened on a large and far extending tract bounded by green hills. In this apartment most of the members of the family – the doctor among them – were sitting about noon, the sun streaming beautifully through the thin, transparent air, when suddenly a strain of melody more divinely sweet than any earthly music they had ever heard, rose near at hand. It was the melancholy wail of a woman's voice, in accents betokening a depth of woe not to be described in words. It lasted several minutes, then appeared to melt away like the ripple of a wave – now heard, now lost in whispers – till 'nothing lives 'twixt it and silence.' As the song commenced the dying boy fell into the last agony … As the last note became inaudible, the child's spirit passed away."

"The following striking case is narrated by Mr. F. H. Rooke (Guildford):"

"Some years ago my sister and I had a joint experience, which has been the greatest comfort to us."

"Our mother lay dangerously ill, every nerve racked with rheumatoid arthritis, and both nurse and doctor seemed to think that her sufferings could not last much longer."

"One night about 1 a.m. my sister was sitting up with the nurse (I was sleeping on another landing), when her attention was transfixed by the most beautiful majestic chords, as if every golden note of melody was being played on some heavenly instrument – music far exceeding anything she had ever heard. Turning to the nurse, she said, 'Did you hear that?' 'I heard nothing,' was the answer. At that moment I entered the room saying 'Where does that beautiful music come from?' The music had awakened me out of heavy slumber."

"As we spoke the sounds died away, and on looking at the bed, it was evident to me that the sweet spirit of our devoted mother had passed to other realms to these beautiful strains. Our father, who slept on the same floor as the invalid, and who, we felt, was as entitled as we were to hear the music, heard nothing."

From the foregoing facts, and also as established by the lessons of the Esthete, we may conclude that the power of sound vibrations is revealed in a thousand different ways. As humans penetrate further into the knowledge of the universe and its inner workings, the law that governs it and musical harmony is revealed to us through its principles, as well as in its marvelous effects. It is through it that all the architecture of the worlds, all the forms of universal life, are built and perpetuated. It can be perceived even by a simple experiment. Is it not curious, for example, to follow on the glass or metal plate, when sprinkled with sand and put into contact with a stringed instrument, the geometric shapes, the delicate and complicated designs that result from each note and each chord?

In the study of art, one must not be put off by an apparent aridity which is only superficial. An attentive examination, with a sustained analysis of every esthetic subject, reveals some unsuspected attractions and helps our initiation into the general law of beauty. We can compare this mental exercise to the ascent of a steep and rugged mountain, where each fold of the ground conceals hidden wonders and which, from its haughty summit, makes us discover the overall harmonic effect of the process unfolding under our eyes.

All human beings can and should be interested in this subject matter, because it offers us intellectual joys far superior to anything yielded by false delights.

Even the humblest workman has in his mind a possible solution to the understanding of beauty, and will find ever new resources to perfect his own work. The art of craft is a route to a higher art. Each one works on a particular kind of beauty, but in their ascending goal, all souls flourish in a radiant conception of the universal and eternal beauty.

The dissociation of matter, the interplay of intra-atomic forces give rise to a new science, which, by developing itself, opens to the human spirit wider perspectives on the work of the Cosmos.

We shall soon recognize the mysterious link between thought and will to vibrations, which turn them into their agent in order to build the innumerable forms that populate the immensity.

In a nutshell, sound, rhythm, and harmony, are all creative forces. If we could calculate the power of sound vibrations and measure their action on fluidic matter, their way of grouping the atomic vortexes, we would touch one of the secrets of spiritual energy.

At least, it suffices for us to observe, in the experiment just quoted, the geometric figures created by the human voice or the bow of a violin on the glass plate covered with fine sand, in order to understand as a comparison, for example, how divine thought, which is the master vibration and the supreme harmony, can act on all the planes of substance and construct the colossal forms of nebulae, suns, spheres, setting their trajectory in deep space.

The spectacle offered by universal life shows us everywhere the effort of intelligence to conquer and realize beauty. From the bottom of the abyss of life, the being aspires and climbs toward the infinite of aesthetic conceptions, toward divine science, toward the eternal summits where perfect beauty reigns. The splendor of the universe reveals divine intelligence the same as beauty in earthly works of art reveals human intelligence!

Music awakens in the soul impressions of art and beauty, which are the joy and reward of pure spirits, a participation in the divine life with its raptures and ecstasies.

Music, better than speech, represents motion which is one of the laws of life; that is why it is the very voice of the higher world.

It takes supreme beauty of form to express the splendors of a universal work. Poetry and music, we have said, cannot stand mediocrity. However, despite the aesthetic indigence of our time, we must recognize and praise the efforts of some authors who, in their attempts, have come closer to the summits and succeeded in composing works in which a certain breath passes, a radiation of sovereign beauty. Through opera, in particular, they managed to stir in the soul the fiber of generous enthusiasms.

It just so happens that, to give birth, to produce genial works capable of elevating intelligent beings to the summits of thought, to the ideal of perfect beauty, it is necessary first of all for one to create oneself, to build one's own personality and make it susceptible to experience, to understand the splendors of the higher life and the eternal harmony of the world.

What forces, what rays, what consolations, what hopes can be passed on to other souls, if one has in oneself only obscurity, doubt, uncertainty and weakness? What could be expected of skeptical minds, shut to all high impressions, deaf to all voices, to all echoes of the Hereafter?

The esthetic misery of our times is explained by the impotence of the contemporary soul to create an enlightened faith, a broader and higher conception of universal beauty.

Therefore, one should appreciate the exceptions that occur and the impetus of a few authors who still strive to bring judgment back to the regions of the ideal.

But as a new ideal awakens and focuses of Spiritualism light up all over the world, a more powerful reflection of the splendors of invisible life, as revealed by the teachings of our spirit friends, will emerge and develop in human souls. And that will be the signal for a flowering of works, the starting point of an artistic era that will surpass in size and wealth the work of the centuries that preceded it.

There is certainly no doubt that the spectacle presented by the earthly world and human life, with their clashing contrasts, has offered us a sufficiently varied number of pictures, images and scenes – the loves and hates, passions and pains – to inspire strong works, such as the past has left us. But what would these subjects be, rich as they are, if compared to the immense panorama unfolded before our eyes by the Spiritist revelation with its descriptions of life on the spiritual plane? What to think of the vicissitudes of a single human existence next to the vast horizons of the soul's destiny in its ascent through the cycle of ages and worlds? And the joys and trials, the falls and recoveries, the descent into the abyss and the rides upon wings into the light, mass sacrifices that are a redress, a redemption, redemptive missions, a growing participation in the work divine?

Who can utter the powerful harmonies of the universe, a gigantic harp vibrating under the thought of God, the song of the worlds, the eternal rhythm which cradles the genesis of stars and humankinds. Or the slow development, the painful gestation of consciousness through the lower stages, the laborious construction of an individuality, a moral being! Who can show forth the conquest of life, ever wider, fuller, more serene, more enlightened by the rays from above; the march from summit to summit in pursuit of happiness, power and pure love!

These vast subjects are within the reach of us all. In every poet, artist and writer there are unsuspected seeds of mediumship ready to hatch; through them the worker of thought comes into contact with the inexhaustible source and receives his or her share of revelation. This revelation of esthetics, which will be appropriate to an artist's nature and specific type of talent, should become his or her mission to express in forms that will impregnate the souls of crowds with a vibration of divine forces, a radiation from the eternal home.

It is through frequent and conscious communion with the world of spirits that the geniuses of the future will draw the elements of their works. From now on the entrance into the secrets of their double life comes to offer humans relief and enlightenment that failing religions can no longer provide. In all fields the Spiritist idea will fertilize thought into work.

Singing and music, when intimately united, can produce the highest impression. When supported by noble words, musical harmony can elevate souls to heavenly regions. This is what is attained in religious music, in sacred chant.

Song produces a healthy dilation of the soul, a fluidic emission that facilitates the action of the invisible powers. There is no truly effective and complete religious ceremony without a hymn. As the pure voices of children and young girls resound under the vaults of the temples, it emerges as a sensation of angelic sweetness.

But, united with unhealthy words, music is no more than an instrument of perversion, a vehicle of ugliness that throws the soul into low sensualities, being one of the causes of the corruption of morals in modern society.

The sound phenomenon develops from circles to circles, from spheres to spheres, expanding to infinity. It carries the soul on its broad waves ever further, always higher in the world of the ideal, awakening in it sensations as delicate as they are deep, which in turn prepare it for the joys and ecstasies of the higher life.

Its mysterious and sovereign power extends itself over all beings, all nature. Indeed, the law of harmonic vibrations governs all universal life, all forms of art, all creations of thought. It introduces balance and rhythm into all things. It influences physical health through its action on human fluids. It is known that the biblical Saul, in his nervous crises, sent for David, who, by the sounds of his harp, calmed the irritation of the monarch. In all times and even today, musical art has been applied to therapy, and not without result. Such examples could be multiplied.

The harp, with its Aeolian sounds, dissipates our worries, soothes our pains and deliciously cradles our souls. Our European ancestors, the Celts, considered it an indispensable element in the intellectual life. Does not the *Code d'Höel*[19] say, "There are three unassailable things in a free man: the Book, the Harp, and the Sword"?

The greatest of all bards, Taliesin, mysteriously disappears, but for a long time his harp is seen floating on the waters of the enchanted lake. And the echoes of the forest of Brocéliande[20] still resonate at certain hours with the weakened vibrations of Merlin's harp.

In music, our European ancestors saw esthetic teaching par excellence, the surest means of elevating thought to the sublime heights where inspiring genius dwells. The harp played an important role in evocations at the sacred enclosures, and in the contact between the Celts and the unseen people.

Also, the human voice, when it is really beautiful, has intonations of a flexibility and variety that make

---

[19] [Trans. note] *Code d'Höel, Roi de Bretagne* (c. 10th century AD).

[20] [Trans. note] A mythological place in France.

it superior to all instruments. Better than these, it can express all moods, all sensations of joy and pain, from the call of love to the most tragic accents of despair. This is why the introduction of choirs into orchestral music and symphony has enriched art with an element of charm and beauty.

Almost all famous composers have enjoyed mediumistic faculties which allow them to receive the inspirations of the Hereafter, translating, according to their own genius, magnificent conceptions of eternal harmony. Among them, the most remarkable appear to be Beethoven, Berlioz and Wagner.

Beethoven should be considered the true creator of the symphony and his phrasing, in its breadth and beauty, represents the complete musical action. From this point of view, his spirit dominates and will dominate modern music for a long time. We are assured that he has recently dictated to a certain medium a hymn for mediumistic sessions, which will be published shortly.[21]

Berlioz, too, was a great symphonist; among French composers, there is none more difficult to emulate due to his vigorous talent and his prodigious virtuosity. In this ardent, passionate, picturesque music, intention and execution are combined; it

---

[21] [Transl. note] See footnote 14 above.

has the ragged contours and power of the alpine region where the composer was born. It expresses in turn the splendor of the peaks and the horror of the chasms. There is the voice of torrents, the murmurs of the forest, and all the harmonies of the mountain in its striking unity and variety.

I will never forget the profound impression caused on me on first hearing *The Damnation of Faust*. I was little more than twenty years old and, for me, it was thanks to this symphony, that the revelation was made of an unknown, dazzling world full of riches and wonders. Berlioz was too great to be well understood by his contemporaries; like most innovators, it was only after his death that the public began to appreciate his lyrical genius.

As for Richard Wagner, his colossal work is entirely imbued with a thick and heavy spirituality, which borders on materialism like all German genius. But sometimes, from this slightly confused mass, often vulgar and commonplace, spring musical rockets that reach the highest peaks.

Wagner may have borrowed a lot from his predecessors, but whatever he borrowed from them, he made it his own and injected with original and personal life.

Unfortunately, in him, substance remains inferior to form, and in this aspect his work lacks balance and precision. His images and his subjects are earthly; when he wants to populate the spiritual world, it is always with gods wearing a tragic and excessively human mask, semi-material, helmeted and armed creatures, which ride on clouds in search of bloody battles. There is no exception, except for two of his works: the operas *Tristan and Isolde* and *Parsifal*, borrowed from Celtic and Christian legends.

His music, as a whole, remains sensual and does not keep the spirit in the high regions of dreams and beauty. It is because Richard Wagner has worked only for the theater and, in opera, as we have already said, the music is chained to the word and this is sometimes cause of weakness and inferiority. In this lyrical genre, to produce the strongest impression, form and substance must be balanced, complement one anther and remain equivalent. The superb form associated with indigent thought vanishes quickly and leaves only a floating impression, a vague memory.

However, despite these flaws and shortcomings, Wagner's work has its place among the great musical creations. It shows us once more that art belongs to all times and countries, and to no particular place.

However, in music as in all things, France has proved to be a balanced nation: taste, clarity, and measure are the essential qualities of French art.

Between the melodious chirps and almost feminine cooing of Italian music, and the powerful virile sounds of German music, French music holds the middle ground and unites the two opposing schools in a synthesis of grace, strength, and beauty.

The works of Beethoven, Berlioz and Wagner seem to sum up the highest musical inspiration of our time. But the future will see other composers emerge, more aware of the invisible world around us, better endowed with the mastery skills that allow us to communicate with it. They will endow humanity with treasures of art and poetry, the richness and scope of which we cannot gauge now, and which will become an inexhaustible source of joy, truth and beauty to us.

Thought and intelligence arise from the same universal harmony as music, and that is why music alone is able to express thought and intelligence's highest and most sublime conceptions, since sound vibration is in itself only a manifestation of universal life. That is why it awakens an echo, in the most secret recesses of the soul; it revives in the latter something like a vague memory of the deep heavens where it was born, where it lived, where it will live again!

SPIRITUAL MUSIC

FIVE LESSONS

After studying earthly music, we will move on to the harmonies of the spiritual plane; and for that I will summarize the instructions given to us by the spirit of Massenet[22] during several seances. In his teaching, the illustrious composer proceeds as he did on Earth, with the same method he applied in his lessons at the Paris Conservatoire.

Initially Massenet will deal with instruments and perception means. But in the spiritual life, these are no longer stringed instruments, or made of copper, as on Earth. The same applies to perceptions, which are no longer localized as in the human body, extending to the entire spiritual body instead.

Earthly music is just a feeble and veiled echo of celestial music; it is the Aeolian melody rendered by heavy and coarse instruments of wood or metal; it is the starry and divine dream expressed by the forms of an inferior and material life. But in this case, the dream becomes a higher reality.

[22] [Trans. note] See Massenet's biography in the Appendix.

If our means of execution, which turned out to be too rudimentary, cannot give us a sharp and clear idea of the supreme harmonies, the difficulty is not diminished when it comes to explain by our usual language the rules and laws that preside over the great eternal symphony. This difficulty has been revealed, above all, in the lessons we have received from the spirit of Massenet, and which will be reproduced hereinafter. As a result, the insufficient terms of our human language are improper to translate all the beauties of the divine work.

To express the sublimities of art, we would need art itself, with its highest and most powerful resources, and most subtle processes.

First lesson of Massenet's spirit

I will try to use the simplest terms and images to make you understand the phenomena of the spiritual plane. When you become disincarnated, you will find that radiations of unequal intensity escape from the perispirit and can reach considerable speeds.

Each spirit, according to its degree of evolution, possesses a more or less perfect vibratory apparatus, that is to say, an instrument adapted to its own self. Material beings emanate fluidic rays that are not very subtle, not etherealized, and whose vibrations are close to nothing. Conversely, in evolved beings the fluidic ray can be compared to a string of one of your musical instruments, very fine, very sensitive and whose vibrations are extremely sharp. The undeveloped being will possess this same string, sounding as if it were soaked in coal tar pitch.

So that is the disincarnate being moving on the spiritual plane now. When its tendencies bring it next to matter, its fluidic rays will transmit only material sensations to the perispirit. But, the more its evolution increases, the more the material sensations diminish and fade away, and its beam of fluidic rays takes on more subtlety, power, delicacy, and softness.

Under the influence of prayer and with the advice and assistance of its guides, this spirit will evolve in an entirely fluidic atmosphere. Its own radiations will meet the fluidic currents of the spiritual plane, and result in wonderful sensations of sound, perceived by its whole being.

Evolved beings live in fluidic spheres, where currents of unequal intensity and diverse compositions prevail. The musical waves are canceled with the immediate contact with your planet, whose fluids are still too materialized. We must climb higher to perceive the chords of the celestial lyre. There are even beings that, from a moral point of view, are perfect, yet still are not able to feel these vibrations.

First, an esthetic education is necessary. I will talk about it soon.

Lesson Comments

by Léon Denis

The human body is a complex and wonderful instrument that adapts itself to Earth's environment and to our multiple needs. Yet this body is only the material, relatively coarse covering of a subtle body, the perispirit, of which Massenet talks to us about, and which we all possess during life as after death.

The existence of this perispirit is demonstrated by the phenomena of exteriorization of the living and by the photographed apparitions of the deceased, often recounted in Spiritualist publications.

This subtle body, admirable in its suppleness and sensitivity, is the imperishable envelope of the soul, and, like the latter, susceptible to purification and progress. It vibrates at the slightest impulses of the spirit and transmits to the physical body the ensuing vibrations, which are necessarily lessened. That is why, on the spiritual plane, during sleep as well as after death, the perispirit feels more strongly the influence of the environments into which it penetrates. It possesses more extensive resources, greater means of perception unknown to humans, of which certain individuals are able to retain intuitive impressions upon awakening, after the soul's release and spiritual journeys during sleep at night.

In this ensemble, which constitutes a human being, the soul or intelligence is the dominant note. The correlation between the two envelopes, the physical and the perispiritual one, refers to a single law, namely, that of vibrations.

The role and functioning of the perispirit remains one of the most interesting issues in Spiritism. It contains in seed form all the secrets of physiology and psychology, which will become clearer as our contacts with discarnate spirits evolve, spread and multiply. Through them we will obtain new data on the conditions of life in the Hereafter and, in general, on the mode of action of the spirit freed from the material body.

Second lesson of Massenet's spirit

Today I will talk, not about the supra-terrestrial instrument as we spirits call it, but about how the discarnate being can move away from the Earth and enter the ethereal spheres where the harmonies of the spiritual world become more perceptible to it. Let us take, for example, a discarnate being of average spiritual education resulting from its previous work and its faith degree.

At the beginning of its life on the spiritual plane, the discarnate being will have to become familiar with its new state so as to be able to awaken in itself the memory of the harmonies that it has perceived in its previous existences. It will feel the desire to re-immerse itself in these harmonic fluids; but from a latent point of view, it cannot immediately know the means of reaching the sphere to which its spirit aspires to ascend. Its spirit guides, higher than itself, make it grasp by intuition and vibrate its perispirit little by little, so that there is no disturbance for the recently disincarnated one.

Thus will be established what we call the concord, and any dissonance will thus disappear between the spirit and the musical sphere where it wants to penetrate. When on Earth you hear an imperfect instrument, if it is not tuned, your poor organs are stunned. The same happens in our life in the Hereafter. The spirit guides impress the perispirit of the disincarnate soul, in order to obtain a more thorough adaptation.

Here then is our subject, now prepared to receive musical waves. As its own radiations connect better with the harmonic beams of the spiritual plane, its yearning grows to rise even higher toward the source of eternal beauty. Once rid of all gross influence, it will go up with its guides to higher regions, celebrating with them the glory of the Most High.

All material fluids volatilize, the perispirit becomes brighter, the radiations more intense, more subtle, and evolution is thus facilitated. The spirit will go up like flying balloons rise in the air on Earth.

Upon penetrating into the higher regions of the spiritual plane, the spiritual being first feels a sensation of gentleness, a sort of expansion, of rapture; then the fluidic rays which emanate from the perispirit come into contact with other ray beams, hence a sort of fluidic shift between two beams of almost equal subtlety, but of different nature. You cannot imagine the impression felt by fluidic beings: they are no longer feelings of well-being, of contentment, but a kind of swaying, of undulation, accompanied by a special sensation, which determines an emotional state, a kind of ecstasy. The vibrations felt in this state form what you call tones: they are produced by the rustling of fluidic layers among themselves.

Higher than these harmonic spheres, there are other regions that I cannot yet reach and where higher beings dwell, creators of sublime music, which is transmitted to us through special fluidic currents. Spirits like me do not perceive the beings that produce it, yet it comes to us through conducting currents of a subtle nature. A spirit guide tells me that the beings that produce the waves of this celestial music are almost perfect and possess a portion of divine genius.

Third lesson of Massenet's spirit

You know how vibrations are formed. The spirit, transported into the vibrational sphere, is enveloped by a network of sound waves whose elements are made up by higher beings. What will you feel! This music will produce in you an impression comparable to that which you experience when listening to the tonic or keynote in music. The more the waves of the vibrational field are developed in speed and length, the more lively is the impression felt by the perispirit, as penetrating and comparable, in human terms, to that provided by high-pitched sounds.

So we have on one hand the tonic and on the other hand the high pitch. If, in the vibrational field, the waves vary in speed and intensity, the amplitude of the sound will vary, and this sounds comes from an initial point, comparable to the tonic. This initial point includes a certain vibrational wave which I am not able to measure. Here is a comparison: Your gramophones emit sounds, where, apart from the sound produced by the instrument, if you approach your ear to the trumpet,[23] you will feel a more or

---

[23] [Trans. note] A trumpet or horn protruded from ancient gramophones before the invention of loudspeakers.

less intense heat, according to the tonal elevation. Well, the discarnate being does not feel heat, but more or less delicious sensations, according to greater or lesser speed, and according to a more or less extended wave.

The radiations which come to strike the perispirit are colored in exceedingly varied hues. Each color has a peculiar property, which gives a sensation of well-being, of satisfaction, which differs according to their purity, the homogeneity of each hue. One must therefore take into account, on the one hand, the quality of the waves – that is, their coloring – on the other hand, their speed, their extent, and the various phases of their convolutions. All this will induce, in the disincarnate being, incomparable and exceedingly varied phenomena, because, the more the spirit is evolved, the more diverse will be the waves that it perceives, as well as the colors expressing the feelings. Take, for example, the color blue, which represents the highest feelings, from an emotional standpoint: A blue wave will give you vibrations that will be for your inner being like a bath of love. Red, under the same conditions, will represent passion. Yellow will be intermediate. Warm pink which is a mixture of yellow and red, will give you a less intense yet more sustained love. So you can, with these fundamental colors, form a gamut of shades which give by correspondence the vibrations of all human and superhuman feelings.

If the discarnate being is still little evolved but has the desire to imbibe beautiful feelings, its spirit guides will lead this spirit to spheres animated with angelic beings. When a spirit is very evolved, it can collect, on the same spheres, gratifications where love and passion will come to impregnate its being, and that is why, back on Earth, beings that love music intuitively can more or less remember their long stays on the spiritual plane, where they were in a field of musical waves.

Celestial music cannot be produced by bowing material strings: everything in it is fluidic, everything spiritual, everything inspired by God's thought.

2nd & 3rd LESSON COMMENTS

BY LÉON DENIS

Already, while on the Earth, the range of sounds as we conceive it, is for us a mere relation of sensitivity which is not absolute. It is well understood that there is a correlation between sound waves and light waves, but such relation escapes many observers and sensitives, because their perceptions are quite different in their degrees of intensity; light vibrations being incomparably faster than sound vibrations.

But for the spirit, whose perceptions are much more powerful and extended, that relation is closer than it is for us, and the sensation is then unified. We have an example of this in the difference between the bass notes, which correspond to darker colors, and high-pitched ones, which correspond to the brightest intensities of light.[24]

Our intelligence, which perceives and sums up all the effects and forms of the eternal substance, embraces all vibrations while itself vibrating through infinity without concern for distances or rhythms.

It is equally easy for us to understand how, in the spiritual life, esthetic pleasures are correlative

---

[24] About this topic, I would like to quote the words pronounced by Mr. Deslandres, director of the Observatory of Meudon (France), in his address to the annual meeting of the Institute on October 25, 1921: "Up to now, 50 octaves of vibrations and waves of the ether have been well recognized and classified. This field of study is much more extensive than that of the sounds perceived by the human ear, which total at most 10 octaves reduced to seven in musical instruments. These 50 octaves are divided into three main groups, namely: the radiotelegraphy group, the group related light waves, and the X-ray group. They are generally arranged in order of frequency, as in a grand piano. On the left, at the low frequencies and bass sounds we find the waves of wireless telegraphy, which provide terrestrial communications systems at long distances. In the center, there is the luminous octave its neighboring octaves which bring heat and light, and let us locate the horizon of a place, the Sun and the stars, and also impress photographic plates and serve to purify water. Finally, on the right, on the side of high frequencies and high-pitched sounds, there are the X-rays, which have remarkable electrical properties that reveal to us the most hidden recesses of living bodies, and the intimate structure of atoms. Note also that, of these fifty octaves, only one, placed approximately in the middle, is perceived directly by one of our senses: it is the octave containing the light rays from red to violet."

to the soul's evolutionary level. On Earth we all have the same auditory organs, yet how different are the sensations experienced by listeners of a symphony, according to one's cultural degree or psychical elevation.

The forms and images produced by sound vibrations in the ethereal spaces, of which the spirit of Massenet speaks to us, to me seem to be further manifestations of the ordering thought which conceived and directed the universe. Celestial music could represent the very vibration of the divine soul. That is why the more the spirit evolves and purifies itself, the more it becomes able to understand, and to feel the beauty and eternal harmony of the world.

Fourth lesson of Massenet's spirit

Today I will speak about sound; not pure sound since we spirits have no ears. Sound is the result of a vibration that strikes physical organs and produces, therefore, a virtual phenomenon.

We must start from this principle: on the spiritual plane, sound is not the sensation caused by a noise, but that which generates a gratification of moral and spiritual well-being. Enjoyment will be more or less intense, and corresponds to the sensations that the instruments on Earth give us.

We have seen the immaterial being transposed to the musical sphere, that is, into the vibratory field animated by angelic beings. We have also seen that this individual being receives, in its perispirit, vibrations which, by sending off their own emanations, will produce sensations of enjoyment.

In human music, you have the **La** as a note of the tuning fork: we will not take this note as a starting point, because its tone does not match the tone of any color. We will take the **Do** (that is, C) instead. The **Do**, in your ears, gives a deep, full sound that expresses joy, a sound that portrays the love we must feel for God. This **Do**, if we make a comparison, adapts better to the first of the fluidic sensations usually resulting in the color blue.

Do symbolizes the blue color of an unclouded sky, the serenity, a soul's peace attained through prayer. **Do** is the first note of the perfect concord deriving from blue.

Mi (that is, the note E) represents strength in love, the will to love, and can be symbolized by a ray of your sunlight. So we have: **Do** and **Mi**. **Do** is fundamentally blue in color; **Mi**, the will in love, will give us azure and gold.

Sol (that is, G), the third harmonic note, represents the consolidation of the two preceding notes or, in other words, a connection that emphasizes the two previous ideas, an emphasis which ensures the externalization of the feeling given by the blue.

We spirits perceive this latter note as a special hue, whose color I will try to convey through your senses, in order to make you understand it. It is neither a ray of silver that could be confused with gold, being absorbed by it; nor a black ray, resulting from other colors that could absorb blue. But it is a shining, colorless, well-defined fluid that can get closer to the radiant light that escapes from the orbs you are able to perceive, that is, blue-gray, silver-gray. Your sun, seen from afar, has this aspect.

The first tone, as seen by a mortal, will have this aspect: a blue keynote. Intensity of the keynote: gold. Stress or duration: silver gray, mixture of blue surrounded by gold and silver gray.

This first tone represents divine love. The other basic colors show all the other feelings, from light yellow to deep red, but these colors present themselves always with their accompanying golden coats and silver-gray peels.

In human music the perfect chord is: Do, Mi, Sol. Starting at Re (that is, D), the perfect chord will be: Re, Fa, La. Starting at Mi, the perfect chord is: Mi, Sol, Ti (i.e., B). The tonic will vary in color from blue to red, but the other two notes will always be gold and silver: these will not vary.

Depending on the quality of one's perispirit and the nature of the vibrational field, sensations vary and increase in intensity, to the point of becoming marvelous. Some perispirits receive yellow, others red. There are some who exclude the latter color.

Violet is less bearable for evolved beings. Light green is more pleasant than dark green. One can, according to the laws of the spiritual plane, perceive a mixture of blue and pink.

Vibrational fields can also vary in intensity. They result from angelic emanations, inspired by the divine being. When we return to Earth, we are still imbued with these vibrations, the material body cancels them, but our consciousness keeps their impression.

Outside these vibrational fields, there are spheres, and even currents, which provide less evolved minds with harmonic pleasures, sometimes vivid and profound, though more personal. These fluidic currents communicate to the self the intimate joys of divine love. Other currents only give it the joy of hearing the chords of the celestial lyre. These vibrations, unstained and invisible to disincarnate beings, yielding them a satisfaction comparable to that derived from the sensation of perfumes.

Celestial music is therefore the result of impressions induced by fluidic layers, according to the elevation of beings and the degree of purity of the ambient environment.

On the spiritual plane one hears nothing; we feel the harmony of fluids and not that of sounds. The essential property of fluids is color. Sound is an earthly essence, whereas color is of heavenly essence. In the next lesson I will deal with the harmonic delights of the spiritual world and their persistence in human feelings.

Lesson Comments

by Léon Denis

The interdependence of sounds and colors referred to by the spirit of Massenet has been glimpsed by all great musicians. One of them said, "Melody is to light what harmony is to the colors of the prism, that is to say, the same thing under two different aspects, melodic and symphonic."

Plato once said, "Music is a moral law. It gives soul to the universe, wings to the mind, flight to the imagination, a charm to sadness and life to everything. It is the essence of order that leads to all that is good and beautiful, of which it is beautiful, but nevertheless passion in an eternal form."

We might note, in passing, that Massenet was rather a melodist than symphonist. To form the white light, complementary colors should agree, and this light becomes all the more lively and radiant as the melody sums up and better synthesizes the harmony of complementary harmonies.

It seems, then, that there is a perfect agreement between the conceptions of earthly geniuses and the teachings of Hereafter entities, while recognizing that these latter give us details and insights ignored by the specialists of our world.

The relations between melody and harmony are like those between thought and gesture. It could also be said that, in music, melody represents synthesis and harmony, analysis. They penetrate each other and are only worth as much as they can combine and merge more completely.

On Earth, the beauty of a musical work results from both conception and execution, but in the life of the Hereafter, the initial idea and the work execution merge because thought communicates to vibrations the fluidic qualities that are unique to it. The work is all the more beautiful, and the impression produced by it all the more lively, the higher is the intention behind it. This is what lends harmonic properties to ardent prayer, to the cry of the soul towards its creator.

The higher one climbs the scale of relations, the more unity appears in its sublime magnificence.

The law of musical notation regulates everything, and its rhythm cradles universal life. It is a sort of radiant and divine geometry. The human alphabet, like the beginner's stammer, is one of its most rudimentary forms. However its manifestations become more and more extensive and important at all levels of the harmonic scale.

The human spirit cannot rise to the supreme heights of art whose source resides in God; still it can at least raise its aspirations to them.

Esthetic agreements are infinite; but it is scarcely in times of ecstasy and rapture that human thought sees some aspects of the universal law of harmony. The musical rule occurs on the spiritual plane in lines of flame; the thought, the expression of divine genius, and the stars in their course, conform to its vibrations.

If the human spirit, in its impetuses, can rise for a moment to these heights, it falls powerless to describe its beauties; the impressions it feels can only be translated by a mute adoration. The spirit of Massenet himself considers itself insufficiently evolved for ascending to these higher spheres.

Once again, one finds here the impossibility of expressing superhuman ideas in human language. Whatever one may say, one always remains beneath the truth. The infinity of ideas, scenes, images is challenging to the limited resources offered by our earthly vocabulary. Indeed, how can we summarize and encapsulate in words all the splendors of the works that unfold in the depths of the starry skies.

Fifth lesson of Massenet's spirit

As a conclusion to my presentation of musical art in the spiritual world, I will try to make you understand the harmonic sensations felt by spirits in the spheres where we live. In my last talk, I referred to the currents induced by angelic beings. I still have to tell you about **wave trails** *(an expression collected from the medium's brain, who happens to have some knowledge of wireless telegraphy). I will* *therefore take, as a comparison example, wireless telegraphy, for it can give you some idea of these harmonic waves I will talk about.*

Lastly, you asked me about the music of the spheres, so here is the explanation: Forces directed by higher wills produce a fluidic current whose vibrational power is considerable but uniform. These waves then travel an immense distance and will impress less advanced spirits than those which can approach the musical spheres I have spoken of. These less advanced spirits have at least, through their perispirits, the faculty of feeling certain undulations. Upon striking these beings, which exist in great numbers, these waves, according to their speed, give a vibration which is expressed in all perispirits by a deep illumination. Any spirit meeting this current on the spiritual plane will feel its perispirit change color! It assumes a more vivid tint, according to the intensity of the current emitted, and thereby will feel adequate gratification with the coloring. As in general these wave trails or currents are caused by feelings emanating from almost angelic or divine beings, you can conceive them as comparable to baths of azure that should extinguish and do away, as far as possible, with passions which are remnants of matter. If there is sufficient will on the part of a spirit that can perceive them, that spirit will be able to derive great benefit from these waves, since they are a form of transmission that can help its elevation, as they all emanate from divine regions.

These currents often revolve around worlds, purifying their atmosphere. When they start from a different point, these currents take on distinct colors that can be confused and determine a double sensation. This explains what some spirits have told you that, on the spiritual plane, "You can hear lyres vibrating."

In general, the tone remains the same, the word 'tone' being taken in the sense of color. For us, color expresses the sensations collected by thought. But many beings remain insensitive to these currents, due to their insufficient progress. There are some that prefer the sensations produced by old carnal passions and thus seek them; others, touched by these currents, ask by prayer to penetrate into spheres where ecstasy is more habitual.

You know that, in the spiritual world, the planes are diverse, but God has allowed all beings to be aware of its benefits. The enjoyments felt are not comparable to those you might have when looking at a beautiful picture or listening to a piece of music: sensations are much more complete and not mechanical like yours. Your terrestrial music is the result of more or less violent impacts on metal, or a slip of air through a sound substance, whereas spiritual music is translated as sensations whose range is propagated through colored degrees! Each color, each colored beam hitting the perispirit, transmits impressions to it which are more or less high and pure, according to the high nature of the spirit which receives them, and according to the intensity of the fluidic waves themselves.

Therefore earthly music is not comparable to spiritual music. The first yields satisfaction of which your nervous sensitivity can profit; the second, which is of divine essence, provides moral joys, sensations of well-being, and ecstasies which will be all the deeper as the receptacle, that is to say, the individual disrobed of a carnal envelope, becomes purer itself.

Final Comments

by Léon Denis

The study of Spiritism in its relation to art is confined to the greatest problems of thought and life. It shows us the ascension of living beings on the scale of existences and worlds, toward an ever wider and more precise conception of the rules of harmony and beauty, according to which all things have been established in the universe. In this magnificent ascent, intelligence grows little by little, the germs of goodness and beauty deposited in it should develop at the same time as its understanding of the law of eternal beauty expands.

The soul eventually becomes able to execute its own personal melody on the thousand octaves of the immense keyboard of the universe. It penetrates the sublime harmony that synthesizes the action of living and interprets it according to its own genius. It tastes more and more the felicities that arise from possessing beauty and truth, and which can be glimpsed by real artists from this world already.

Thus, the way of heavenly life is open to all, and all can walk through it through their efforts and merits, attaining the possession of those imperishable goods that the goodness of God keeps in store for us.

Therefore the sovereign law, the supreme goal of the universe, is in itself beautiful. All problems regarding the question of being and destiny can be summed up in a few words: Every life should be the putting into action and full realization of beauty, the fulfillment of the law.

The being that has arrived at a lofty conception of this law and its applications must help all those that lie beneath itself on the climb of this magnificent scale of ascents.

Lower order beings, for their part, should work to secure material life and make possible the necessary freedom of thought for thinkers and researchers. This commonality of interest ensures the immense solidarity of beings, united in common action.

The entire ascension of life toward the eternal summits, and all the splendor of universal laws, can be epitomized in three words: Beauty, Wisdom, and Love!

Appendix
Biographies

LÉON DENIS
HIS LIFE AND TIMES

When the true Codifier of Spiritism, Allan Kardec, suddenly died in Paris in 1869, it soon became clear to most that his best immediate continuators were Gabriel Delanne (1857–1926) and Léon Denis (1846–1927).

While Delanne devoted his efforts to the scientific side of the new body of thought inaugurated by Kardec, Léon Denis explored above all its moral and philosophical aspects. Both have written incessantly and later gained international recognition, with Sir Arthur Conan Doyle, no less, translating Denis into English for the first time. This he did with utter dedication and conviction, as revealed in his preface to Léon Denis's *The Mystery of Joan of Arc* (London: Murray, 1924):

"Until one has experienced it one can hardly realize the difficulty which lies in the adequate translation of a French book, dealing with a subtle and delicate subject. Only then does one understand that not only the words, but the whole method of thought and expression are different. A literal translation becomes impossibly jerky and staccato, while a paraphrase has to be very carefully done, if one has a respect for the original. M. Léon Denis has given me an entirely free hand in the matter, but I love and admire his book so much, that I earnestly desire to reproduce the text as closely as possible."

So who was Léon Denis, after all?

Born in a small French village called Foug, on January 1, 1846, he was forced to quit school very early in order to earn a living and help sustain his family, which was very poor. That would not prevent him from developing his dazzling intellect and an extensive culture which come forward in nearly every line he wrote, besides, of course, an impressive command of his mother tongue.

He got in touch with Spiritism for the first time when he was 18, while reading Kardec's *The Spirits' Book* (New York: USSC, 2016). Two years later he met Allan Kardec in person, during one of the latter's promotional tours of France.

By the 1880s, Denis had become one of the main contributors of *La Revue Spirite* [*The Spiritist Review*].[25]

---

[25] The book *Spiritism in the Arts* first appeared as a series of essays in the Parisian journal *La Revue Spirite* throughout the year of 1922.

"A full and steady faith can only be acquired through slow and painful initiation," said his spirit guide to comfort him in his darkest hour, when he was surrounded by hostility and incomprehension, coming even from his own family, despite his minor but important military successes as a low-ranking officer before the age of thirty.

However, even in the army, his experiments with spirits did not seem to stop:

"A sergeant of my company was a medium, so I took him to this house on a winter night, and we both sat at a table, with the intent of solving the mystery behind these manifestations. The table was soon agitated and then overthrown by an irresistible force. Pencils were broken; the sheets of paper, torn. Raps shook the walls; deafening sounds seeming to come from beneath the ground were heard. Suddenly the light went out. A rumbling, stronger than all the preceding noises, made the house tremble, then faded away in the distance, in the silence of night. Before leaving this haunted house, we learned that it had formerly been the scene of bloody episodes."[26]

Life was never easy for Léon Denis. Maybe that is why one tends to disregard some contradictions and biased opinions referring, for example, to France as a nation and culture, and its people, which would otherwise seem quite offensive to other countries and languages. Yet a genuine generosity of heart and solidarity with those who suffer was a strong,

---
[26] L. DENIS, *Into the Unseen* (New York: USSF, 2017), p. 240.

positive trait in his character that completely offset such matters.

When it came to literature, Denis proved to be quite modern and adventurous as an art lover, while keeping an entirely conventional profile regarding music and painting. So while mentioning writers such as Baudelaire and Gérard de Nerval in the same exalted breadth, he would totally ignore the greatest musical genius that France has ever given the world: his exact contemporary, composer Claude Debussy (1862–1918).

Instead, we have the traditionally "safe," but still brilliant, Jules Massenet as a teaching spirit. In fact, it is Massenet's contribution that turns *Spiritism in the Arts* into a unique document about music composition and execution in the Hereafter.

Léon Denis became an accomplished orator while still in his twenties. This helped him enormously later on in the dissemination of Spiritist teachings, especially in France and Italy, but also in Algeria, for he traveled a lot after a certain age, uniting the useful to the pleasing in his new job as a merchant.

Many decades later, after publishing a series of books and giving talks in some of Europe's most respected societies and institutions, he was invited as president of the *Congrès Spirite International* of Paris in 1925 to speak before a large audience packed with the most renowned savants of the time. In the end, much to his surprise, they gave him a standing ovation.

LÉON DENIS, AGE 79, CONGRÈS SPIRITE OF PARIS, 1925

That was a fitting send-off for a man who had devoted his long and strenuous life to the Spiritist cause with unswerving conviction.

A SELECT BIBLIOGRAPHY

LACHAPPELLE, Sofie. *Investigating the Supernatural: From Spiritism and Occultism to Psychical Research and Metapsychics in France, 1853-1931* (Baltimore, MD: The John Hopkins University Press, 2011), pp. 46–47, 76.

LUCE, Gaston. *Léon Denis, l'Apôtre du Spiritisme* (Paris: Editions Jean Meyer, 1928).

Jules Massenet
HARDWORKING COMPOSER

Very talented, but not a genius, he was the most popular French composer at the end of the 19th and beginning of the 20th century. Of his thirty or so operas, only two – perhaps three – continue in the repertoire today, namely, *Manon* and *Werther*. The third one would be *Thaïs*, though it survived mainly as a concertante piece for violin and orchestra.

However, when Léon Denis wrote *Spiritism in the Arts*, the music of Massenet was still much appreciated; and there can be no doubt that his name generated a certain frisson among Spiritists and sympathizers, when it was announced as the second spirit to contribute valuable insights and information to the study at hand.

Indeed its lessons are the most revealing, articulate and focused of the two communicating entities, reflecting a real concern for clarity and accuracy. Many a pupil had been impressed with Massenet's didactic prowess while he was still here on Earth.

Like Denis, he had very humble beginnings. Born in Montaud (Loire, France) in 1842, he was sent to the Paris Conservatory at the tender age of ten by his loving mother, who was an amateur musician and his first tutor.

Already a composer in his late teens, he won the coveted Prix de Rome, which granted him a scholarship in the prestigious French Academy in Rome, Italy. The fine portrait by Chaplain, illustrating the frontispiece of this biography, comes from this period.

Soon, he would establish himself as one of the last composers of Romanticism, especially with operas, oratorios and songs; and a prolific one at that.

His first success came at the age of 35, with an opera mostly forgotten today, *Le Roi de Lahore*.

After that, he knew international fame and fortune, with eleven productions of various of his operas in New York alone: "A record probably which no other composer besides Wagner could boast of in recent years," said the *New York Times* on August 14, 1912.

In his extraordinarily candid autobiography, *My Recollections* (Boston, 1919), translated into English by his personal friend H. Villiers Barnett,

Massenet revealed that his mother had given him an unusual gift on his tenth birthday:

"Here is a diary ... every night before you go to bed, you must write down on the pages of this memento what you have seen, said, or done during the day."

And so he did, keeping this habit all through his life, which greatly enriched his memories as he climbed up through joy and sorrow.

When he first published his memoirs, *Mes Souvenirs* (Paris, 1912), in what proved to be the year of his death, Massenet had been diagnosed with cancer two years earlier.

MASSENET PHOTOGRAPHED NEAR THE END OF HIS LIFE

The last chapter of *My Recollections* caused surprise and even astonishment at the time. In it the composer speaks to the reader as if from the Hereafter, even stating at one point that there is no death and the soul is immortal.

The following excerpts are taken from "Thoughts after Death," the truly uncanny final chapter of Massenet's *My Recollections*:

"I have departed from this planet and I have left behind my poor earthly ones with their occupations which are as many as they are useless; at last I am living in the scintillating splendor of the stars, each of which used to seem to me as large as millions of suns ..."

"An evening paper (perhaps two) felt it to be its duty to inform its readers of my decease. A few friends – I still had some the day before – came and asked my concierge if the news were true, and he replied, 'Alas, Monsieur went without leaving his address.' And his reply was true for he did not know where that obliging carriage was taking me ..."

"At home, Rue de Vaugirard, my wife, daughter, grandchildren and great-grandchildren gathered and almost found consolation in their sobs ..."

"And my soul (the soul survives the body) listened to all these sounds from the city left behind. As the carriage took me farther and farther away, the talking and the noises grew fainter and fainter, and I knew, for I had my vault built long ago, that the heavy stone once sealed would be a few hours later the portal of oblivion."

H.M.M.

A SELECT BIBLIOGRAPHY

MASSENET, Anne. *Massenet and His Letters: A New Biography* (Trans. M. Dibbern, Hillsdale, NY: Pendragon Press, 2015).

MASSENET, Jules. *My Recollections* (Trans. H. Villiers Barnett, Boston: Small, Maynard & Co., 1919).

PHOTO CREDITS

P. 129: LÉON DENIS, circa 1870, photographer unknown
P. 133: LÉON DENIS, 1925, Agence Rol
P. 135: JULES MASSENET, 1864, crayon by Jules-Clément Chaplain
P. 137: JULES MASSENET, photo by Nadar (Gaspard-Felix Tournachon)

www.ingramcontent.com/pod-product-compliance
Lightning Source LLC
Chambersburg PA
CBHW061658040426
42446CB00010B/1798